EFFINGHAM
C O U N T Y

EFFINGHAM
COUNTY

TRANSFORMING THE ILLINOIS PRAIRIE

F. Delaine Donaldson

Charleston · London
THE History PRESS

Published by The History Press
Charleston, SC 29403
www.historypress.net

Copyright © 2010 by F. Delaine Donaldson
All rights reserved

Back cover, top left: Courtesy of the Mason Civic Center, Mason, Illinois.
All images are from the author's collection unless otherwise noted.

First published 2010

Manufactured in the United States

ISBN 978.1.59629.965.8

Library of Congress Cataloging-in-Publication Data

Donaldson, F. Delaine.
Effingham County : transforming the Illinois prairie / F. Delaine Donaldson.
p. cm.
ISBN 978-1-59629-965-8
1. Effingham County (Ill.)--History, Local. 2. Effingham County (Ill.)--History--19th century. 3. Effingham County (Ill.)--Biography. I. Title.
F547.E4D66 2010
977.3'796--dc22
2010030903

Notice: The information in this book is true and complete to the best of our knowledge. It is offered without guarantee on the part of the author or The History Press. The author and The History Press disclaim all liability in connection with the use of this book.

All rights reserved. No part of this book may be reproduced or transmitted in any form whatsoever without prior written permission from the publisher except in the case of brief quotations embodied in critical articles and reviews.

CONTENTS

Preface   7

Part 1. Establishing a County on the Prairie   9
The Native People Living on the Prairie—Griffin Tipsword, First Settler—Ben Campbell and Other Early Settlers—The Cumberland Road and Civilization's Advance—National Road Towns—Ewington and Freemanton—The Honorable William Blakeley's Role

Part 2. From Settlement Until the Outbreak of the Civil War   26
The Allsop Story—The Growth of Ewington—The Growth of Freemanton—Local Lore About Abraham Lincoln—Saddlebags Doctor: Medicine on the Frontier—The H.H. Wright Story—The William Wilson Story—Outlaws on the Prairie—Establishing the Faith Community—Early Churches in Effingham County

Part 3. The Civil War and Effingham County   47
The Establishment of Railroads—St. Joseph's College—A Saintly Visitor from Aachen to Teutopolis During the Civil War—Effingham County During Civil War Days—Soldier Stories—A Divided Public—Civil War POWs—The Mary Newcomb Story: Following the Troops into Battle—Benson Wood, Politician and Orator Extraordinaire

Contents

Part 4. Effingham County During the Latter Nineteenth Century   72

The Effingham County Courthouse—Outlaws and the Railroads—The Development of the Local Media—Governor Altgeld's Visit, October 13, 1896—William Jennings Bryan on the Courthouse Steps During October 1896—Dr. Wright's Mansion at Altamont—Dr. James Newton Matthews, the Poet of the Prairies—Lewis H. Bissell: Genius in Photography

Part 5. Effingham County, Early 1900s Until Mid-Century   94

The Great German-Catholic Convention in 1907—Effingham County and the First World War—The Liberty Bell's Visit to Effingham County—Dealing with the Great Depression—A Night of Horror: The St. Anthony Hospital Fire and Triumph of Spirit

List of Sources   119
About the Author   127

PREFACE

Reminders of history come in many forms. There are written records, of course, but there are also reminders in old photos, in stone or brick buildings, in monuments chiseled out of granite and in imprints on metal. Whatever the form, however, when a person looks at the visible record, the mind is taken back to another day when people long since deceased lived and breathed and contributed to the way life is lived today.

These reminders are best described as "mind-flints," items that spark interest in the person who sees the object. Effingham County is dotted with those reminders of the past, the fascinating events that happened many years ago. This book is based on the "mind-flints" that the author observed while traveling through the countryside or while perusing the archives of the Effingham Historical and Genealogical Society, newspaper archives found in area libraries and nineteenth- and twentieth-century local history books.

As such, this work is not an exhaustive history. It is a mere sampler of the rich heritage of the prairie county whose citizens see themselves as "The Heart of the USA." The intent is to spark interest that will lead the reader to seek out more information about the people and events that are described in the following pages. If the old adage "A picture is worth a thousand words" is true, the text represents only a small portion of the whole history. The reader should seek out the rest of the story.

PART 1

ESTABLISHING A COUNTY ON THE PRAIRIE

Along the highway on which the traveler journeys between Watson and Mason, in Effingham County, there is a metal sign that serves as a "mind-flint," sparking remembrances of a time long before there was any permanent settlement in the 480-square-mile county. The sign points us backward to a time when there was an ocean of grass where nomadic native tribes roamed, maintaining their way of life on prairieland abundant with all types of animal life. The people were the Kickapoo, native people who would soon disappear from the central part of the state as white settlers displaced them. There are limited glimpses into their way of life by way of artifacts (arrowheads, spear points and the like that they left behind), burial mounds and insights offered by explorers and settlers who followed them.

For instance, the journal entry written by surveyor Joseph Shriver for Sunday, July 13, 1828, contains a description of "an Indian adventure," a phrase sometimes used to refer to the practice of native tribes in nearby Clark County swooping into a camp whooping and hollering, generally trying to frighten the explorers but without having any intent of doing them harm. Most white people did not appreciate the Indians' sense of humor.

Shriver and people like him learned a lot from the way the native people used nature as a cure for common diseases. Later physicians in Effingham County respected the medical knowledge of the native people. Dr. Frank W. Goodell, who practiced medicine during the late nineteenth and early twentieth centuries, wrote:

Native prairie grasses near Mason along Illinois Route 37.

The Kickapoo Indians were here when the first white man came. They had their "medicine man." He was shown honor and esteem by the Indians, as they lived in their tribal relations. They were men of sense and judgment… They studied under a preceptor, and taught their science and art, to whom their mantel was to fall. To learn was a plain case of memory. They were scientists and did not know that. They were the most practical of botanists, but never saw a botany [book]. They would walk out in the woods or prairie and select plants whose leaves, bark, roots, or berries they wanted. They had to know their habitat, their color, height, their petals, corrola, radix, stamen, pistils, or it would be impossible to make a differentiation, on which would determine the poison and the non-poison and the dosage. Practically all these plants were given in infusion, which would be as reliable and practical as our "fluid extracts"… They used the quirkus for diarrhea, bitter bark for tonic, Phytolacca for rheumatism, Lobelia for asthma, Podophyllin for cathartic, tobacco for anti spasmodic anti septic pountices, tannin, soot, and pressure to control hemorrhage, sweating or cold to reduce fever, bathing in hot or cold water for cleanliness, they knew Belladonna, Sanguinaria, Serpentaria, and they used a narcotic, but I do not know what it was.

Establishing a County on the Prairie

Broken bones they adjusted, surrounded "the false point of motion" with moss of soft grass, and applied a splint to the parts, which consisted of a piece of bark, cut from a tree the proper diameter to correspond to the "dressing," and this applied contracted around the parts, held in place by strings of skins…

Death from childbirth among the Indians was as uncommon as it is now in our greatest age of culture. The late Rev. Dr. W.H. St. Clair told me, he saw an Indian woman hidden in a clump of bushes, while some braves were fighting, and three squaws came down to the opposite side of the river, the one delivered, leaned against a tree, and supported herself by holding to a swinging wild grape vine. One squaw manipulated and the other stood waiting to help while the "papoose" was being expelled. When born the mother lay down on the grass, and the afterbirth was removed by her dusky accoucher, the umbilical cord having been ligated twice, and severed between the ligations. The baby was washed in the flowing water of the river. Its eyes, anus and sexual organs were carefully and minutely examined. Who could have done better? When Dr. St. Clair arrived home, he said his wife ran out excitedly to meet him, and said "O William, I do wish you'd been here a little sooner. An Indian woman was just here, showing her baby, and begging, and honest, William it didn't seem it was more than three hours old," and the doctor replied, "It wasn't." The mother had walked three or four miles, and her companion had carried the baby.

When Reverend Alfred Bliss, Methodist circuit rider and Effingham land developer, talked about his family moving into the region in the late 1830s, he said that native tribesmen came to the windows of his house, pressing their noses against the glass because they had never seen such windows before. They were not threatening. The white settlers had no reason to fear them—most of the time.

By researching another historic reminder from early Effingham County history, a stone monument in Summit township, a person can learn about social relationships between the native tribes and the white settlers. That monument sits atop a hill well above Wolf Creek where Griffin Tipsword, a veteran of the Revolutionary War, resided. His presence in the area showed that permanent settlers were going to move into what would become Effingham County. The year was either 1814 or 1815. An explorer much like the famous Daniel Boone, Tipsword took up his residence with the Kickapoos, for he was a roving nomad just as they were. He was a man who wanted plenty of space in which to live his life. He joined the Indians in their hunting, their conversations, their dances and ceremonials, so much so that his life was a blend of white man's civilization and Native American culture. In fact, he married a Native American. Due to his close relationship with the Kickapoos, he presented his oldest son to the Indians so that they might educate the youngster in their way of life.

Tipsword's life story is an adventurous one. He left Virginia in 1812 to travel to the southern part of Illinois, where he remained for two or three years and then moved northward with his wife and two children into this south-central part of what would become the state of Illinois. Just like the Indians, he seemed to follow the game as he looked for a better place to hunt. For nearly sixteen years, his relatives had no idea what had become of him. But the local tribesmen knew him. He was a doctor, a preacher and a pioneer.

Burial site of Griffin Tipsword near Wolf Creek.

In his practice of medicine, Tipsword often used what he had learned from the native tribes. It appears that his patients were much impressed with his great skill. To the very end of his life, he maintained many of the customs and practices of the native people who were living here. Long after the Indians had left the area, Tipsword was still a resident, and when they often returned annually to hunt, he would go with them.

This earliest white settler also knew about potential conflict as the two dissimilar cultures came into close contact. After white people had settled in nearby Shelby and Fayette Counties, some of the Indians decided to massacre all recent arrivals, hoping to destroy all whites from Shelbyville to St. Louis, including the people who lived in Illinois's capital city, Vandalia. Many white settlers in the area were terrified. They had no idea what to do, but they had been warned that they must leave within three days. Into this great difficulty Tipsword entered, going to the general meeting that the Indians scheduled in a wooded area. Although he was there as a spectator, his early days in Illinois had prepared him for a most vital role. The first of the speakers

Establishing a County on the Prairie

urged that the adult males adorn their bodies in readiness for war and then attack the whites who lived in the area. Many of the young men agreed. Later in the evening, when Tipsword spoke, he was able to persuade them that although they had the power to kill all the whites, such a massacre would bring the army of the United States government into the area, and with that, all Indians would die. The highly respected frontiersman's description was so persuasive that it brought talk of a massacre to an end.

Griffin Tipsword died in the year 1845, leaving behind surviving children John, Isaac and Thomas. Standing near his grave site in Tipsword cemetery on the banks of Wolf Creek, the student of local history senses the adventuresome spirit of a man who, because he shared the experience of two cultures, was a bridge between a people who had lived for generations as traveling nomads and a people whose settlements would soon permanently alter the Effingham County prairie.

There were other daring frontiersmen who soon left their marks on the area's history. William Henry Perrin's 1883 *History of Effingham County* tells the story of many of the settlers:

> *Fifty-seven years ago, 1825, Mr. Scott, in company with a man named Elliott, and his wife, traveled through this county on their way, moving from Wayne to Shelby County. They camped near Blue Point. In passing the timber at the head of Brockett's Creek, a smoke was seen curling up from a camp fire, a clearing, or a wooden chimney. Mr. Elliott, who had made the trip through here before, told him that it was smoke from the cabin or clearing of a man's place named Fancher. This was Isaac Fancher. That Fancher was here then is strongly corroborated by the oft-repeated statements of Ben Campbell to his stepson, Thomas Andrews, that when he [Campbell] came here in 1825 he found the Fancher family here; that he stopped with them for several weeks, and they put in their time hunting bee-trees, of which they found a great many. Campbell also stated that he thought the Fulfers were here when he came, or that they came soon after.*
>
> *This brings up the record of early settlers to 1826. It is brief and soon told. Griffin Tipsword and family, 1815. Isaac Fancher and family, 1825. Ben Campbell, and Jesse and Jack Fulfer, 1826. And John O. Scott, and Elliott and wife passing through here as movers in 1825. Fancher and Fulfer in 1834–35 moved away from here into Coles County, where they died years ago. With the exception of Mr. Scott, these, the earliest of the pioneers in our county, are all gone—sleeping peacefully in their unmarked graves.*

EFFINGHAM COUNTY

In 1828, Thomas I. Brockett and family, and Stephen Austin, Dick Robinson, John McCoy, Bob Moore and Richard Cohea came. In 1829 came John Broom, Jonathan Parkhurst, Ben Allen, Mrs. Charlotte Kepley, Jacob Nelson, Andrew Martin, Alexander Stewart, John Ingraham, John Trapp, Samuel Bratton, John Fairleigh, Alfred Warren, Amos Martin, and old Aunty Bratton, Andrew Lilley, Henry Tucker, William Stephens, Allec Stewart, Bill Stewart, and Jacob Nelson.

In 1830, Jesse Surrells, T.J. Rentfro, James Turner, John Allen, Micajah Davidson, Henry P. Bailey, George Neavills, Alexander McWhorter, Jesse White, Enoch Neavills.

In 1831, Jacob Slover, Isaac Slover, John Gallant, William Gallant, Seymour Powell, Thomas Loy, William J. Hankins, the Hutchisons, and John Galloway, the fiddler.

Here were the fifty-one families that were here prior to February 15, 1831—the date of the act of the Legislature organizing the county. Why did they come? What was it that stopped here this meager stream

Nineteenth-century Summit township homestead.

of emigration and fixed them permanently in this place? What was there here to tempt and lure them to brave all, endure all, and cause them to fix here the nucleus around which all this present people, and their wealth and enjoyment has gathered? True, they could not see the toils and danger that lurked unseen upon every hand, yet there was much to repel them that they could see, enough, one would think, to have settled the question, and forever have prevented them from flying in the face of dangers that they knew not of.

An especially colorful early settler was Ben Campbell. Just like Tipsword's, Campbell's story shows that these early pioneers' experiences were the stuff of which legends are made. Again, Perrin's book records:

Ben Campbell…one of his kind. A man of tremendous physical organization, with coarse features, a sun-burned skin, that was covered with hair and unsightly "bumps" all over his face; great scars upon his face and body, especially a frightful scar that ran down the whole left side of his cheek, injuring the muscles of the eye and giving it a strange expression. Sandy, coarse, stubby hair and beard, blue eyes, very large mouth, with thick lips, and teeth double-rowed and so large that they looked more like horse's than human teeth. Generally dressed in skins of animals he had slain, except a small, close-fitting red bonnet that was always on his head. Altogether a figure well calculated to frighten children to death, and might even appall timid grown people when suddenly beheld for the first time.

While hunting one day, he met an Indian who had a splendid fresh deer skin on his shoulder. By a strange coincidence Campbell had a bright silver half-dollar in his pocket. Campbell much wanted the skin and the other coveted the money. Negotiations resulted, and the hide and half-dollar were placed together on a log, to be fought for by the two men.

Campbell always wound up his story by stating that for nearly an hour he could not, for the life of him, tell whether he was going to get the deer skin or loose the half-dollar. But he eventually got it and walked off with his trophy.

At one time he went to Vandalia when the Legislature was in session. On his way he killed a fine fat turkey-gobbler. This he negotiated at the hotel for his dinner and horse feed, stipulating that he was to have his dinner earlier than the regular meal and to have some of the turkey. When he sat down to the table he ate the entire turkey, as well as everything else that was on the table. Mother Maddox, the landlady, declared that she honored the guest that honored the food she put before them by eating heartily, and so she extended a life-time invitation to Campbell to always come, and, without money and without turkeys, to eat at her table free…

Campbell was a man who was moved in everything by his own promptings. He knew little or nothing of the rules of society, and he cared less. He was an honest man, and as rough of speech as rough could be. He was crabbed, sullen and moody of temperament. A stranger seemed to affect him as a red flag does a mad bull. Such he would generally roughly insult without cause, and while he was slow of speech and his words were few, he could make his taunts sting terribly. If the stranger, in ignorance of the man, resented the insult, a fight was improvised at once; and in the old style of rough-and-tumble-knock-down-and-drag-out, he seldom met his match. Yet, the fight once over, he was ready to drink friends at his victim's expense—get roaring drunk and savagely friendly.

He lost his pioneer wife, and after awhile he made up his mind to marry again. He had heard of Robert Moore's widow in the northwest part of the county. He had never seen her, but, nothing daunted, he mounted his horse and rode to her house, called her to the door, and as he sat upon his horse, looking closely at the widow, he finally informed her that he had come to see her on business—that he wanted to marry her—but that she wouldn't do, and he turned his horse and rode off. He proceeded to another house, where there was also a widow, called her to the door, told her his business, and commanded her to mount behind him and go to the magistrate's and be married. The poor woman remonstrated and begged for time; but with oaths that fairly snapped as he uttered them, he told her to mount, and she mounted, and the cooing doves rode off and were married.

His death, on Christmas Day, 1856, was much after the manner of his life. He not only died with his boots on, but on horseback. He had been to Freemanton all day and in the evening started home—one of the Higgs boys riding behind him. When the horse stopped in front of his cabin door, Campbell made no motion toward dismounting—he was dead.

Other early residents of the area established scattered settlements throughout the territory that would become Effingham County, but their presence did not account for much population growth until the United States government provided a thoroughfare to the West—the extension of the Cumberland, or National, Road into Illinois. This first federally funded highway was truly a monumental cultural achievement with major significance, commercially and politically, for the geographic areas through which it passed.

Establishing a County on the Prairie

One historian wrote, "The Cumberland Road was a symbol of Federal power, and a bond of union. It drew attention to something that the Nation was doing, rather than the States." When, after 1825, politicians began to explore the possibility of the road connecting the capitals of the western states—Columbus, Indianapolis and Vandalia, and eventually the capital of Missouri—a nearly thirty-year constitutional struggle began. Henry Clay, famous for his "American System," became the oratorical champion of the Road in the West. When he spoke at Wheeling, West Virginia, on March 31, 1829, the Kentucky statesman declared that the road should be "protected, repaired and preserved by National authority" because it "is a Bond of Union" connecting two great sections of the country. He stressed the obligation of the national government to control all aspects of the road rather than turn over the maintenance to what he regarded as inferior local jurisdictions.

The continuation of the Cumberland Road into Illinois was no easy task. Lieutenant T.S. Brown, the engineer who conducted the official inspection of the road in 1833, wrote of his appreciation for those who were charged with building the Road: "The task of constructing this road in Illinois was one of no ordinary kind, and was not to be executed with credit to the superintendent, or to the satisfaction of the department, without the greatest zeal and industry, joined to professional attainments, practical and theoretical, of an elevated order." From a plethora of difficulties, one factor dominated: there were few people in the four-county region. In fact, in the late 1820s there was only one house between the Indiana-Illinois border and Vandalia. Consequently, no readily available supply of workers existed to complete the necessary tasks. There was a need for persons with high degrees of mechanical skills and for supervisors with the ability needed to select quality building materials in an area where few quarries existed. Also because of the limited settlement of the area, there were few roads over which to transport the materials needed for an effective and long-lasting roadway. The absence of settlement meant that there were few banks. Superintendent William Greenup had to travel to St. Louis, where there was a Branch Bank of the United States, in order to get the money needed to pay the contractors.

Another difficulty stemmed from the superintendent's concern for keeping road costs at a low level. Greenup granted contracts to those who presented the lowest bids. Such a practice did not contribute to construction quality on the road. Lieutenant T.S. Brown indicated that, in 1833, the masonry work was of poor quality on culverts and bridges, that foundations were insufficient, that walls were weak and that clay or mud was used for mortar.

His general assessment was that storms and other natural forces would cause the structures to deteriorate rapidly. Some of the poor quality of workmanship stemmed from the dishonesty of contractors who were motivated to protect themselves from loss by slighting the work, while some shoddy work was done by individuals who simply were ignorant of quality work standards. Because the superintendent had to focus much of his attention on monetary accounts, many of the masonry works were completed by inexperienced people without any real supervision. In contrast to the masonry work, the wood on bridges was sufficient to meet federal standards, although Lieutenant Brown felt that the work in general was not of any real benefit to the government. Whatever the official analysis, the work on the road changed the lives of the generation who contributed to its construction and to the people of subsequent eras who lived their lives along the Cumberland Road.

Work began in Clark County in 1827 through 1828 when axe-men began cutting a path through a wilderness occupied by large numbers of deer, wolves, panthers, wild hogs and a few bears. Almost immediately, people became aware of the job opportunities, so laborers started to move to the unsettled Illinois counties. These workmen were a diverse lot. Some, like John Hix, former regimental commander of a group known as "Hell's scrapings" who served under General Wayne, were veterans. Some, like Scotsman Alexander McGregor, were immigrants, while others were simply people seeking whatever opportunities were available along the route. Some became squatters; others built hotels or any of a variety of businesses related to life on the road.

There was need for supervisors, or local superintendents, but by far the greatest need was for manual laborers who would clear the roadway for the grand project. Arriving in covered wagons, workmen often brought their families, who would live in the wagon until a cabin could be built. Many workers on the road settled near the route, while others moved on when work halted.

Although many immigrants regarded the road merely as a stagecoach route, there was an active pioneer life that developed near the road. There was an abundance of wild game, which provided meat for the table. Crude cabins, as well as taverns and hotels, were part of the frontier in Illinois. Life was unsophisticated and primitive.

Axe-men were busy in Effingham County by 1829. As was the case in Cumberland County, Effingham County was not organized until after the Cumberland Road passed through the area. In 1831, the year of organization, the population consisted of only three hundred persons. At the same time, the workforce on the road numbered approximately the same as the permanent residents.

Establishing a County on the Prairie

Diversity characterized the workers. One was an Irish immigrant who had run out of money as he traveled to the West. Another was a black laborer who met an unfortunate end when he got caught in a blizzard and froze to death as he attempted to walk nearly thirty miles from his cabin near the Little Wabash River to Vandalia, Illinois's capital at the time. The work settlement consisted of a supply store and a variety of crude, unhealthy pens and sheds that housed the fairly sizeable workforce engaged in the construction of a bridge across the Little Wabash River. The bridge project was an expensive but poorly done job that soon washed away. Local people quickly seized the opportunity to carry away the stone abutments to wall up wells and provide foundations for private buildings. Although the work efforts produced short-term effects on the area, the concentration of population and the potential for commerce was such that nearby Ewington became the first county seat.

There were not a lot of trees to be removed in Effingham County. The main feature of the landscape was the tall prairie grass, which had to be cleared so that the roadway was visible. Again, the efforts did not provide long-lasting results. Stage drivers who used the road had to focus on a distant object that had been identified as a landmark in order to be sure they were still on the roadway. At Altamont, there was an intersection with tall cottonwood trees that served as a guide to the travelers.

It was in Effingham County, just a short distance west of Ewington, that the Cumberland Road came to a practical completion. From that point on, there was only scattered work at streams all the way to Vandalia. The lack of congressional appropriations simply did not permit the development of the road at the level experienced in the states farther east, although the official terminus of the National Road was Vandalia.

Complaints about the road were abundant. One traveler wrote, "Everything has grand appellations but in reality is nothing but wretchedness." Another echoed related sentiments: "I was very proud of the Jehuship with which I threaded the intricacies of the 'National Road.' I have since driven across the St. Gothard Alps; but this was the more difficult feat of the two." The negative sentiments reflected the problems of the natural characteristics of the land and of the hardships related to the construction of the road. The former, although essentially beyond human control, presented challenges to anyone who contacted the road.

The oceans of tall prairie grass, tall as a man on horseback, contained many horrifying perils, as well as bountiful blessings. Prairie fires eighty to one hundred miles in width could frighten the most daring adventurer, while great swarms of insect pests, like the prairie flies, could make life miserable for humans and beasts alike. The abundant numbers of "greenheads," as the flies were called, were matched by the thousands of prairie chickens, partridges and blackbirds that were easily startled by the traveling immigrants.

The road was used by thousands looking for a better life for themselves and their families. The would-be settlers carried few belongings. Typically, their covered wagons held a limited amount of furniture, a few dishes, some cooking utensils, a limited quantity of work clothing, sundry farm tools and some bed clothing. Usually accompanying the settlers were some livestock—oxen, cows and sheep.

Travel was slow and confusing. One English emigrant who needed to have his family's luggage returned from Vandalia to Terre Haute due to a change in plans found that it took a man and a boy seven days to make the round trip between the two towns in order to retrieve the desired goods. Because of the tall grasses, travelers found it difficult to determine where they were. Distant, but tall, trees were used as guides to stay on the roadway when it seemed to blend into the prairie. Trees were also used as devices for marking the main road. Three notches in the trunk of a tree indicated that the wayfarer was still on the main road. Local residents marked county boundaries by clearing the bark on a tree and then putting the first letters of the county name on the tree.

Whatever problems may have existed, however, the road proved to be a well-traveled route. In addition to the settlers, freight lines, competing with one another in terms of speed of delivery, accommodations and tariff rates, were regular users of the route. For the farmers, the route was a valuable link with markets such as St. Louis. Unfortunately, the cost of transportation nearly consumed the value of the goods being transported. For the government, the most important use was as a post road for the U.S. mail. By 1846, the Illinois towns and villages along the Cumberland Road—Marshall, Lodi, Martinsville, Casey, Greenup, Woodbury, Teutopolis, Ewington, Freemanton, Howards' Point, Cumberland and Vandalia, all part of the postal system—served as means by which interior America maintained contact with the coastal regions.

Stagecoaches played a vital role in the mail service and in the passenger service. Twice every day traveling each direction, the stages were an important part of Illinois life. The stage stops were located approximately every ten miles where fresh horses were obtained. At nearly every stop, there were taverns to accommodate the travelers, where for twenty-five cents a person could get a bed and a meal. The quality of the Illinois inns was poor. In addition, typically travelers felt that the mud in the spring and deep ruts in the summer and fall made the road a nightmare to travel. No matter, though, for economically, politically, socially and culturally, the Cumberland Road changed forever the nature of life in nineteenth-century Illinois.

The economic impact of the highway had many facets to it. First, there was the money generated by salaries and wages paid to the workers. The road was an expensive project. Congress appropriated tens of thousands of dollars each year for the continuation of the route west. As a result of the availability of the money, businesses that catered to the road workers experienced great success, as did those that provided goods and services needed by the federal government. Later on, these same businesses continued to prosper as travelers used the same inns, hotels and taverns. Seeing the opportunity for wealth, land speculators platted towns and villages along the route. The speculators bought the land at relatively low prices and then sold at rates that provided a good return for each dollar invested.

Until the railroads began to cross the countryside, the road was the "great commercial artery" for the West. The people of the region had access to the cities that were developing in Indiana and Missouri. By traveling the road, the frontiersmen could go to Terre Haute or St. Louis in order to buy and sell. Sometimes representatives from the city businesses traveled the Cumberland Road to make purchases from the rural areas. For example, in St. Louis, there was a branch office of the American Fur Company whose agents traveled through Effingham County and on to communities in Cumberland County to buy pelts. In one season, one settler sold one hundred coonskins to the traveling purchasing agent.

The "artery" had many territorial "veins" that also were important for the local economies. Roads led from the Cumberland Road to the more remote settlements; hence, people from the older communities were linked with people who were new to the region. In similar fashion, the various villages on the road became connected economically. Within the four-county area, for example, residents of the Greenup area traveled to Woodbury and Teutopolis to shop for goods not readily available in their locality; likewise, the road served as the connecting link between the counties through which the route passed and neighboring counties. By 1836, a road was laid out between Newton and present-day Effingham.

The peopling of the area was also important for economic development. Many towns, or villages, owed at least part of their reasons for existence to the fact that the road was located in the county. The Cumberland Road was the most used land route in the westward migration. As a consequence, the counties through which it passed tended to grow each decade in the mid-nineteenth century. In 1830, for example, Effingham County had only approximately 300 residents; by 1850, there were 3,792 people living there.

Population growth such as that stimulated in part by the Cumberland Road's construction always has had political ramifications in Congress and in the Electoral College, but there was another political impact of the roadway. The road was the determining factor in the location of the seat of government. That fact was shown early in Clark County's history and then, again, in Effingham County. The location of the work camp near the Little Wabash River dictated the location of Ewington, the first county seat.

There were also important social effects of the road. In a positive way in those communities that had newspapers, the local media published lists of all unclaimed letters in the different post offices in the state of Illinois. In that way, travelers could maintain communication with their family and friends who remained in the East. There were negative effects as well. Disease, so commonplace on the frontier, affected roadwork and travel. For some of the illnesses, there were simple solutions; other health problems were not so easily dismissed, however. A constant threat on the frontier was cholera. In 1855, an epidemic of that disease in Effingham County struck a wagon train seeking the National Road. Several travelers going through Mason, south of Effingham, were fatally stricken. When death occurred, the deceased's companions buried them next to the roadway.

There was also an unsavory characteristic of social life along the road. In several of the villages, there were transient, lawless groups who frequented the taverns, drinking heavily and gambling extensively. At other locations, taverns seemed to serve as hideouts for horse thieves who traveled the road by night. There was a need for civilizing influences.

Two historic reminders of the building of the National Road, on which work had started in 1829, are the cemeteries at Ewington and Freemanton. In the first location, there is a metal marker that commemorates the location of the settlement. In the second, there is a cemetery containing the graves of many early settlers of the town that disappeared. In both settlements, there was a clash of a "Wild West" type of culture with one characterized by more stable values.

Although the next chapter will be devoted in greater depth to describing the settlement of early villages, it is helpful to have a limited knowledge of the establishment of what became the county seat and of one highly respected citizen.

When the federal government commenced work on the National Road in 1829, a considerable force was stationed at the Little Wabash, engaged

Establishing a County on the Prairie

Brass plate commemorating the first county seat of Effingham County.

in building a bridge across this stream. Workmen's shanties, described as "rude, miserable pens," were built by the workmen. No matter what the quality was, however, these workers, as well as the first circuit courts, utilized the buildings as temporary resting places. The community was located only twenty-nine miles from the state's capital city, Vandalia. It was an elevated site surrounded by timberland, looking over the bottomland of the nearby river, which sometimes flooded and inundated the town.

Ewington, the original county seat of Effingham County, was laid out on the land donated to the county by Joseph and James Duncan for public buildings. Surveyed and platted September 5, 1835, by William J. Hankins, county surveyor, the little town was named for General W.L.D. Ewing, one of the first lawyers who practiced in the county.

A visitor to Ewington Cemetery first notices a tall white monument that marks the burial site of William Blakeley, a man who was a great defender of the National Road, but his story is far greater than that one aspect of Effingham County history.

When Blakeley died at his residence near Effingham on Friday morning, July 5, 1878, he left behind an interesting personal history. Born in New York in 1808, after growing to adulthood, he traveled west on horseback,

The Ewington Courthouse. *From* Fiftieth Anniversary Souvenir of Effingham, Illinois, *1903*.

arriving in Effingham County shortly after it was organized. He entered into business in Ewington and for forty-four years was an active, upright and honored citizen of the county. For many years he was a merchant, but in later years he was most generally known as a large, thrifty and successful farmer.

Beginning in 1839, when Mr. Blakeley was appointed clerk of the circuit court by the judge Sidney Breeze, he began a career of public service that included being a member of the National Road Convention, which met in Terre Haute, Indiana, to appeal for greater congressional support for the road. In 1847, he was a member of the Illinois Constitutional Convention. He represented the district composed of the counties of Effingham and Clay, a post which allowed him to assist in framing the Illinois Constitution of 1848. In 1852, he represented the same counties, plus the addition of Cumberland, in the General Assembly. That body was responsible for

Establishing a County on the Prairie

Ewington Cemetery grave site of William Blakeley, National Road advocate.

amending the charter of the Illinois Central Railroad, a change that greatly influenced the future prosperity of the state.

His obituary stated: "In 1872, after twenty years of private life, Mr. Blakely [*sic*] was again elected by the legislature by the counties of Shelby, Cumberland and Effingham. Although one of the oldest members, he was one of the most industrious. His seat was never vacant and whether in the committee or on the floor, his constituents always had a watchful, earnest representative."

PART 2

FROM SETTLEMENT UNTIL THE OUTBREAK OF THE CIVIL WAR

The economic and social development of the Illinois prairieland in Effingham County is an interesting story that deals with the creation of a civil society in a time when many people wanted to live lawlessly. The story of the process by which a stable society came into existence is found in a closer look at the early communities, the people who lived there and the institutional change brought by the communities of faith that soon sprang up in the heartland of Illinois.

The history of the county's transformation from open prairieland to an area dotted with settled villages deserves a detailed account. In a delightful book entitled *Prairie Boy*, a descendant of an early Beecher City area settler, whose surname was Allsop, described the family members' arrival at the land claimed by the father. Bleached buffalo bones marked the corners of the property. Mr. Allsop explained to his children and wife, "The buffalo have gone farther west. But they left their bones on the prairies. This grassland was their home for hundreds of years. The surveyors and I found their traces everywhere."

Prairie Boy's author so eloquently described what the new settlers were doing. These early settlers never even "dreamed they were part of a great movement of peoples that would result in the settling of thousands of acres. The prairie grasses had waved for thousands of years. Neither fires nor herds nor ancient people had subdued it." But now the land was being transformed. Homesteads were a major part of the process.

Settlement along the National Road covered a wide tract of land because the earliest inhabitants all built their dwelling places near the wooded areas.

From Settlement Until the Outbreak of the Civil War

Pleasant Grove cemetery marker along Moccasin Road.

They knew that the timberland would provide the needed building materials, as well as fuel for fires to drive away the cold of the wintertime. Living by the woods also seemed to provide protection from the terror of grass fires and the dreaded greenhead flies.

As mentioned, the village of Ewington resulted from a work camp for those building the National Road. Businesses soon joined what had originally been only a cluster of cabins. William H. Blakeley, who had opened a store a little farther west, near the present village of Funkhouser, saw opportunity for profit when the county seat was laid out and became the seat of justice of the area, so he moved his store to the new town. His business lasted for a number of years. The next stores were kept by Judge Parks and Judge Gillenwaters. After them came a fellow named Lynn, who opened the largest stock of goods yet brought to the town. Other stores followed as they were needed, and Ewington became quite a business town.

Many enterprising individuals sought to provide services found in other frontier towns. Eli Cook opened the first tavern, and Samuel Fleming, well known as a pioneer tavern keeper of the county, opened a second. Later on, Charles Kinzey constructed a hotel. The 1883 county history described the building as "marvelous in its metropolitan character, and…elegant and sumptuous." Although Kinzey realized that the rough little town was a backwoods community, he was determined to bring a lifestyle to the Illinois National Road in keeping with his own. This fancy hotel finally came to an end when it burned to the ground, giving rise to rumors that, because the rather colorful owner had a great many enemies, the destruction may have been something more than an accident.

Other buildings in the town housed a variety of enterprises. Charles Gilkey opened the first "grocery," although to many residents it was simply a "whisky shop." A post office was established about the year 1835, with William J. Hankins as postmaster, justice of the peace, surveyor and clerk of the court. There was, of course, a school, originally located in a room of a private residence. By the 1850s, a schoolhouse had been built in connection with the local Masonic fraternity. It was a two-story affair, with the Masons using the upper story as a lodge room and the school being located in the lower portion of the building. In keeping with the times, there were buildings associated with transportation: a horse mill and a carding-machine and a few blacksmith, wagon and other shops. Taken together, these composed the community.

Although Ewington was bustling with development during the 1830s, the town was not officially incorporated as a village until April 10, 1855, followed by the election of the first board of trustees. When Thomas Loy, clerk of the court, administered the oath of office to D.S. Mitchell, H.H. Wright, A.G. Hughes, W.T.N. Fisher and Josephus Scoles each swore to "support the constitution of the United States and of this State, and…[to] discharge the duties of trustees of incorporation of the town of Ewington to the best of [his] ability," and further, each man swore he had "not fought a duel, nor sent a challenge to fight a duel, the probable result of which might have been the death of either party, nor in any manner aided or assisted in such duel, nor have been knowingly the bearer of such challenge or assistance since the adoption of the constitution, and that [he would] not so engage or concern [him]self directly or indirectly in or about any such duel during… continuance in office. So help me God." The board then proceeded to elect D.S. Mitchell as president and B.F. Kagay as clerk. A few days later, W.T. Myers became the assessor, while Thomas M. Loy was elected treasurer, with J.H.I. Lacy as constable.

Some of the town's residents and visitors had interesting stories to tell about the little village. Especially interesting are those that became part of the local Lincoln lore. During his adult years, Joseph Horn, one of the earliest settlers of Teutopolis, related that during the 1840s, when the courthouse was at Ewington, it was the custom for many people to travel to the county seat to view the trials, simply for some activity to fill their time. They went to see the judges and hear the lawyers argue against one another. Horn said that in one fall term of court in the late 1840s, Abraham Lincoln and Judge Thornton came to Ewington, traveling on horseback.

From Settlement Until the Outbreak of the Civil War

Unfortunately, Lincoln had torn his coat on the trip and did not want to appear in court in such clothing. The man who would become the "Great Emancipator" sought a tailor upon his arrival at Ewington, but the town did not have one, so the struggling young lawyer was directed to Joseph Horn, a court spectator who, most importantly, was a tailor at Teutopolis. Lincoln borrowed a replacement for the torn coat, which Horn took home to mend. For the rest of his life, Horn talked about the fact that he had patched the coat of Lincoln. Other settlers testified of the same.

Other parts of Ewington's history did not have such excitement. Although the trustees were faithful in their attendance at regular meetings during the first year, they soon became lax, gathering without concern for punctuality and then without concern for meeting at all. On February 7, 1857, three years prior to the transfer of the county seat to the city of Effingham, the trustees met for the last time.

When the center of county government relocated to the village of Effingham, many of the early settlers moved there as well. That new location, although about the same size as Ewington, had excellent prospects for growth due to the fact that it was situated on the Illinois Central Railroad. As a result, within less than a generation the first county seat was merely a series of dilapidated buildings, a mere ghost town.

Four or five miles west of Ewington was another National Road town. Today, the only visual reminder that a town existed at all is the Freemanton cemetery. When entering the burial grounds today, a visitor can literally walk on the earth over which one million people traveled westward along the Road, many of migrants making the trek toward the land beyond the Mississippi River.

Settlement near Freemanton began at approximately the same time as that at Ewington, i.e., about 1830, that being the earliest date of entries of land purchases in the United States Land Office for that locality. Riley Howard was the first to secure land near the future town. Most of the first settlers in the area, however, were not landowners but were men who helped build the National Road. When the federal government suspended work on the road, in 1834, these laborers decided to establish permanent roots for their families. It was then that people like William Drysdall, Christopher Radley, Henry Job and Isaac Lackey secured land, became actual settlers and built homes for themselves, joining earlier residents the Freemans, John and William, whose family provided the name for the town.

On April 18, 1834, Robert Peebles obtained from the federal government the land that became the town site. Soon thereafter, he transferred ownership

The depression entry to Freemanton Cemetery is the original National Road.

of the land to John Freeman, who in rapid fashion met all the official demands needed to create a town. On June 21, 1834, William Hankins, county surveyor, certified that he platted the town of Freemanton, the first town to be platted in Effingham County.

Quickly thereafter, a United States post office was located in the village. At this location, mail coaches traveling the National Road stopped for relay and mail delivery. The postal service at Freemanton served a wide area, extending even into Fayette County.

The wife of the local postmaster had an interesting event in her life that also became part of the local Lincoln lore. In her book, *Vandalia: Wilderness Capital of Lincoln's Land*, Mary Burtschi wrote about an incident involving Abraham Lincoln and Matilda Flack, wife of Milton Flack, one of the first surveyors in Illinois and the postmaster at Freemanton:

> *Accordingly, the Vandalia Hotel was a gay place when the General Assembly was in session. In the candle-lighted rooms of the inn state officers, lawmakers, men of influence, and their ladies attended parties, cotillions, and banquets.*

From Settlement Until the Outbreak of the Civil War

Unquestionably Lincoln frequented the inn, but only one incident is actually recorded of his presence. The youthful legislator attended a party in the hotel one evening. His shabby appearance and unbecoming manners according to feminine standards were major shortcomings that Vandalia belles could not easily overlook. Lincoln was aware that the local young ladies were avoiding him so he asked Matilda Flack, wife of Milton and a relative of the proprietor, to dance. During the frolic Lincoln stepped on her dress and tore it. His great concern at the mishap counterbalanced his awkwardness. He was so personable and genuinely sorry about the unfortunate incident that Matilda Flack could not be disgruntled with the unhappy young man.

More settlers continued to move into the area during the late 1830s and early 1840s. By 1843, the settlers at Freemanton and nearby decided that their community deserved recognition as a voting precinct. When the county surveyor at the time presented a petition to the Commissioners Court asking that body to grant the desire of the citizens, that petition was approved and the boundaries were fixed. Shortly thereafter, the first election at Freemanton took place on October 2, 1843, with Charles Bogges, W.W. Young and Richard D. McCranor serving as first election judges. By the time of the election, the little town boasted of several businesses: a blacksmith shop (which, incidentally, made the first steel plow in the country), a store, a mill and a few other economic ventures, as well as a post office. By 1850, the mill had steam power. Economic success seemed to be in the air.

By the mid-1840s, James Devore and Jacob Bishop, both licensed preachers in the Methodist Episcopal faith, organized a congregation at Freemanton and began to have regular church services. The first building for worship used was a log structure built at the east end of the village, near the cemetery's location.

In 1846, when the Mexican War broke out and there was a call for soldiers, Freemanton proved its loyalty by meeting its quota. When the war ended, those veterans who returned soon saw more evidence of prosperity. John C. Defenbaugh opened a general store in the village that sold products of every sort—silk goods, ox yokes, ox bows and bow pins.

The business boom continued through the 1850s. In the middle of that decade, John M. Brown bought the Bishop mill and decided, after a couple of years, to transform it into a factory for making plows and other farm implements. But then the Civil War came, and the Freemanton plow factory was brought to a permanent halt as men answered the call to volunteer for military service.

The settlement witnessed nearly one hundred of its own entering the field of battle in the years from 1861 until 1865. The prosperity that had characterized the village dried up as the town was nearly depopulated by the war effort. Four years after the war, when the Vandalia Railroad was built, that important business venture was located about a half-mile from Freemanton. Adding insult to injury, in 1871, the village of Altamont, about four miles west, came into existence, soon becoming a thriving town. The result was that Freemanton was almost entirely abandoned, with everything movable taken away. Soon the village plat was vacated and the lots were turned into farmlands. Only the cemetery remained.

Physicians also appeared in the prairie towns in those early days. It was not an easy life. Patients had to be visited day or night by the doctor going to their houses on foot, horseback or in a carriage. There was not a road into many parts of the county for several years, and then only "a cart road" that a doctor had been responsible for building. Carts could travel quite well on such a road if drawn by one horse, but if two horses pulled the cart, there could be trouble. A doctor on horseback could travel on either side of the middle of the road, selecting the best side. But even then, the doctor had to keep dodging and ducking to avoid the limbs of trees. Whatever the circumstances, nothing on earth was equal to the saddlebags thrown over the doctor's saddle.

During the nineteenth century in the small towns in Illinois, the singular figure who dominated the local scene in matters of culture and leadership was the community's physician. From being a role model in clothing style to acquainting the townspeople with classical literature, the small-town physician played a role unlike anyone else.

All members of the doctor's family participated in the crucial leadership function. For the spouse, there was a need to live up to the position: Catherine Goodell, wife of Dr. William Sherman Goodell of Effingham, Illinois, in her latter years and in anticipation of her death composed a lengthy note to her children and then pinned it to the flyleaf of one of her Bibles. In her obituary, a local newspaper copied the note exactly. In part, it read:

> *The theme of my life has been to upbuild humanity, to improve at whatever cost, trying to attain the higher life. I have read only good books—scientific, historic, and religious. Can repeat from Burns, "Awake My Saint John," "Alexander Selkirk on the Isle of Juan Fernandes," "Mary in Heaven," "Lord Byron's Prayer," many stanzas from "Childe Harold's Pilgrimage," Byron's "Ode to Tom Moore," several from Longfellow, etc., etc. I have*

From Settlement Until the Outbreak of the Civil War

> *heard lectures from Agasis, Bayard Taylor, Barnum, Gough, etc. Heard Lincoln speak on politics. He and my husband had a discussion. Heard Douglas nearly the same time...When I was married, I found my education not sufficient for my position, so I resolved to study—became proficient in botany, philosophy, and could read Latin considerable.*

For the physician's children, there was encouragement to excel. For example, Dr. William Goodell's (the Goodells moved to Effingham shortly after the conclusion of the Civil War) son, Frank, although the family was Presbyterian, attended Effingham's German Catholic school in order to learn the German language. Accomplishing that task, he enrolled in a subscription school taught by a Presbyterian minister. Finally, he enrolled in the local public schools, all the while receiving at home instruction in anatomy, chemistry, physiology, etc.

Life, in general, was rough on the Illinois frontier during Effingham County's first two or three decades. In an unpublished manuscript, H.H. Wright gave insights into that roughness experienced by those who lived in the little towns as he recounted his remembrances from his youth. The following excerpt is edited for spelling and grammar:

> *My father had bout 80 eighty acres of land adjoining Ewington which had a horse mill and several log cabins. After he died, mother moved into the cabins and we tended the mill. We ground corn, some little wheat and buckwheat. We had to bolt by hand. Forty bushels was the biggest I recollect grinding in one day. Every man furnished his one team. Those that had but one horse would join with his neighbor and a good many had oxen. Some come 15–20 miles. It would take them two days to get their grinding and get home if they had good luck. My brother who was 3 years older than me did not like the mill and mother would help me often repair the mill. This was along the 1837 and about that time mother had a big hued log house built and a big log stable and put out a sign on a pole, "Travelers Rest" and her name. Then on the day, I was fourteen years old, I was sworn in to carry the mail, and I started out the same week. The route was from Vandalia by the way of Martinsville, Ills. then to Palestine...Well I carried the mail to Palestine three months and the route was to another party and went from Vandalia to Terre Haute, Indiana and twice a week. The party that had the contract then name was Cavanaw lived seven miles East of Greenup, Ills. I had put up at the house. They kept what we call a tavern. The old man was not able to do any business. He died with the*

Edgewood Cemetery burial site of William Wilson, chronicler of early county life.

> *consumption in a short time and the widow Cavanaw rode out to Ewington thirty-two miles to see mother and to hire me. She gave me twelve dollars a month. Her son, a man grown, was on the east end of the route. We met. I took his mail and he mine. We had to ride only four days in a week. Well that did not last long till it was made a stage route. There was a four-horse coach. There was a stage stand at my Mother's called "the Widow Wrights" and also at the Widow Cavanaw's. I was too small to drive four horser. That was in '38. I was 16 years old then while I was carrying the mail on that last route the Government put an express on from Terre Haute through to St Louis; and they went ten miles an hour.*

An adult perspective on life in Effingham County during the early transformational years came from the pen of William Wilson, who settled near Edgewood. After arriving in Illinois in 1852, Wilson, skilled in quarrying and related stonework, began a journey southward from Chicago. His destination was an Effingham County location known as "Dismal," a place where a former acquaintance was seeking workers to help clear away brush for the Chicago branch of the Illinois Central Railway. Recounting many

From Settlement Until the Outbreak of the Civil War

hardships along the way, including injury and difficulty in finding places to lodge at night as he traveled to the place that seemed to signify the misery of the frontier, Wilson arrived in Ewington, lodging with Sam Fleming. The next day, he made his way to the area where the work was available. He had the contract of all the stonework and was getting ready to commence work.

Wilson described his experiences in an unpublished manuscript using his own spelling. He wrote about the problems related to getting enough skilled workers to quarry the rock, as well as the need to secure stonecutters and masons and other "workers of all descriptions." Once a large work camp was created, the next problem was that of obtaining enough wholesome food to take care of the crew, since area farmers grew only enough food for their own families' subsistence.

Workers experienced homesickness for families left behind. The laborers began to talk about bringing those loved ones to the area. Letters were exchanged between spouses. For Wilson, word came that Mrs. Wilson was headed to Ewington via Terre Haute, Indiana. After trying to wire his wife, he traveled to the county seat since a telegraph line was in place along the National Road. When he failed in his attempt to send the telegram due to the wires being down, he took the stagecoach, "the first put on at that season, owing to the bad roads." When he found his family, the group began the journey but only with great difficulty. Wilson wrote:

> *About two miles on our way we run in to a chock hole and broke his leaders draw bar and he had to go right back to where we started from to get another. While he was gone we had her pried up out of the hole with some old fence rails which happened to be close by. When he came back we started on again and soon we came to a mud hole and the driver would say, gentlemen I would like you to get out and walk for I have a terrible piece of road to go through, so we had to get out several times and walk from five to 15 rods at a time before we reached Ewington. We made the trip in about 24 hours, so I think we done very well considering.*

Wilson related how his family faced the cholera epidemic that plagued Effingham County in 1855. His description reeks with the terror of the hardship of life on the prairie frontier:

> *In the fall me and my family was all sick with fever and again living in a round pole shanty. I was just able to creep around. I had to pile them all up on one bed and cover them up to keep the rain from them and several of the*

neighbors dying with the cholery. I offered five dollars for a woman to come and wash up some clothing for me and family, but could'ent get one for that the sickness was so bad. The Doctor that was attending my family was in to see them one day and was dead the next, and every body was getting badily scared.

As in many of the Illinois frontier communities, there was also a spirit like that associated with the Wild West in many locations in the county. In several villages along the road there were those who caroused on Sundays, frequented taverns, drank heavily, gambled extensively and had vicious fights. Often, stores in the towns were stocked with few groceries and lots of whiskey. The rowdy behavior frightened travelers who saw the groups gathered in the streets of the towns through which the Road passed.

Outlawry and banditry were commonplace. In neighboring Cumberland County, for example, the "Springpoint Outlaws" preyed upon local farmers, including those in Effingham County. The lawbreakers had an effective plan. First, a lookout visited taverns frequented by farmers, listening for conversations that indicated who had sold livestock, a clear indication of who had a large sum of money. Because reputable banks were practically nonexistent, people took their money home with them, thus creating excellent opportunities for the outlaw band. Next, after the farmer left the tavern, the gang's lookout followed him to determine precisely where he lived. Finally, the lookout notified the rest of the gang, who completed the robbery later in the night. Quite often, the robbers disappeared from the area for a while, living in a place called "The Dark Bend," a desolate place on the Embarrass River between Newton and Saint Marie, in Jasper County. If the legal authorities suspected the robber's identity, friends of the bandit testified on behalf of the accused in order to block his imprisonment. Sometimes, if a neighbor found out too much regarding the outlaws' activities, he was killed.

Similar problems existed in Effingham County near Altamont. A hideout near the Cumberland Road served as a place where horse thieves safely resided until nighttime, when the road was used to transport stolen horses. Similarly, the Radley Hotel in St. Francis Township was well known for its gambling, and violence.

Other parts of Illinois were aware of the problems in Effingham County. An 1881 *History of Sangamon County, Illinois*, a county nearly one hundred miles from Effingham, described a killing near the town named for Ewing:

From Settlement Until the Outbreak of the Civil War

William S. Swaney, an Ohio man, with a large family, a blacksmith by trade, who kept a man working in the shop, and devoted the greater part of his own time to trips abroad in his buggy, being absent, frequently, weeks at a time. It was accepted as general rumor that he handled cards very successfully and that this was the secret of his mysterious journeys. There came a time when he failed to return. Weeks rolled into months, and finally the papers reported the finding of the body of a man who had evidently been murdered, near Ewington, in the east part of the State. The clothing was described quite minutely. The widow visited the place and fully identified the clothing. The body had been dead sometime when found, and was already buried. It was supposed that some gambling comrade, whom Swaney had fleeced, had taken this means to obtain revenge and re-secure his wealth, for no money was found upon his body.

But by far the most notorious criminal act that occurred in those early county days was the killing of Richard Hill in the town of Freemanton. In the 1883 *History of Effingham County*, a connection was made between Hill's death and the previous death of William Swaney:

At high noon, on the 15th day of April, 1842, in the town of Freemanton, Dick Hill, as he sat upon his horse, conversing with Jesse Newman, was shot dead. Hill was in the road and the man he was conversing with stood inside the yard, and near a blacksmith shop. The report of the gun was probably heard by all in the little village, yet to this day it has never been proven who fired the shot. His head, shoulder and body were riddled with buck-shot, and his death must have been instantaneous, as he rolled off his horse and fell limp and dead in the road, where he lay just as he had fallen. Some of the scattering shot had slightly wounded the horse's shoulder, and the frightened, riderless animal running past the few village houses at full speed, toward his home and along the road his master had ridden a short time before. This added to the report of the gun told the tragic story unmistakably to all. When the horse dashed up to his master's door, the empty saddle and the yet warm blood told the frightful story to Mrs. Hill. It was a short half-mile from the scene of the tragedy to Hill's house.

The screams of the woman could be plainly heard, as she rushed out of her door, caught the horse, bounded into the saddle and at full speed started to the village. With mingled screams, sobs and execrations upon the murderers, and waving her hands and arms above her head, she came to where her dead husband lay. The horse stopped when she flung herself to the ground, fell upon the corpse, pushed one hand under the head, and in doing so covered the hand and part of her arm in the dark mud made by the blood, as it mingled with the dust of the road; she raised the head until the face of the living and the dead were nearly along side each other, when the maniac wife and dead husband presented a picture that will never fade from the memory of the few who looked upon it.

The scope of the lawlessness showed that a conflict had arisen; advancing civilization had to cope with the lack of social control. Among the remedies were vigilante action, a police state or self-control. Somehow, the social norms of respect for human life and personal property had to be instilled in those who lived in the four-county region through which the Cumberland Road passed.

In Teutopolis, citizens used vigilante action to solve the problem. A group decided to set a trap for the Springpoint Outlaws. While in a tavern, a German farmer boasted about his good fortune resulting from the sale of livestock. The words were so convincing that the outlaw scout was enticed to rob him that night. To his surprise, a group of nearly fifteen armed men awaited. There was no gold, but lead instead. The problem was solved.

But vigilantism can be dangerous. If the legal system is sidestepped, well-meaning people become threats to the social order. A workable democracy depends on the citizens having cultural values that encourage personal safety. Without such, chaos reigns.

Two basic social institutions, the family and the church, working in tandem with each other, can provide values needed to reduce a lawless spirit that threatens life and property. The family came naturally to the area, being drawn by employment along the Cumberland Road. The church required a bit more effort for its establishment. Both instilled the virtue of self-control and related values.

Frontier churches helped to establish and maintain order in the new communities, a really difficult task due to the character of life along the Cumberland Road. Ministering consisted of two basic tasks: caring for relocated communities and converting people who did not belong to any church and who gave little evidence that they wanted to. As a result, the frontier preacher faced arduous challenges.

Those who delivered the Gospel message to the frontier came from a variety of backgrounds. Roman Catholic priests were highly trained. Some Protestants were as well, but others were self-taught people who felt the need to reach the frontiersmen with the message of salvation.

From Settlement Until the Outbreak of the Civil War

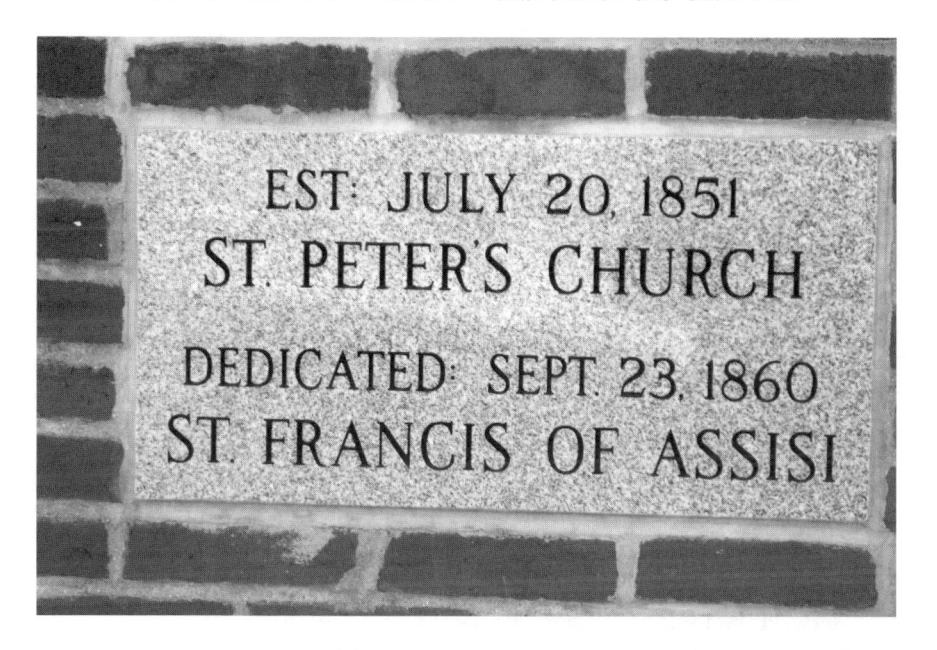

Above: Cornerstone for St. Francis Catholic Church, Teutopolis.

Right: Bethlehem Lutheran Church, rural Altamont.

Effingham County

In the last named category, one especially colorful local figure was Joseph Boleyjack. He and his wife were surely among the most memorable characters to live in Effingham County during the early years. Both left deep impressions on the people who met them. Joseph's first name was rarely used. He was simply "Boleyjack," a man sometimes called "the parched corn, summer preacher," referring to his diet and to the season of the year when he most often "exhorted" his listeners.

In many ways, he was the stereotypical coonskin pioneer. Some said he dreaded soap and water, a trait not uncommon on the frontier. In dress, there was nothing fancy or sophisticated. Instead, he wore a shirt of "coarse, home-made tow linen" and breeches consisting of buckskin in front and rear. And the breeches were always short, with his shins having no covering at all. His head was covered with a coonskin cap, but he rarely covered his feet. On those unusual occasions when he put on a pair of shoes, he wore no socks. Even then, the shoes did not cover his feet; although his toes were not exposed to the elements, "his heels braved the wind and weather."

Like most of his neighbors, Boleyjack used whatever was available in nature for his pioneer clothing. For example, he was quite resourceful in the use of the native hickory trees. Shoestrings, although rarely needed, were made of hickory bark. Likewise, his breeches were "drawn up nearly to the neck by a single hickory bark 'gallus' which was fastened by goodly sized wooden pegs in lieu of buttons." To a traveler unacquainted with the frontier, Boleyjack seemed to have "the appearance of a young shell-bark hickory."

Based solely on appearance, there was no evidence of great talent, yet it was his avocation that defined his life. He knew how to preach! It was said that his fire and brimstone sermons were capable of making "reprobates tremble, women…cry and shout aloud, and many a tough old sinner…fall upon his knees and plead with Heaven in agonizing groans and sobs."

His eloquence thundered through his sanctuary—the woods through which he roamed—preaching a pure and simple Gospel to the best of his knowledge and ability. He was humble and sincere as he warned his fellow frontiersmen about punishment for the unrighteous. He wanted to proclaim that he was "not ashamed of his Lord and Master."

Both he and his wife lived hard, difficult lives in the prairie county. The Boleyjacks' log cabin was floorless and plain. Their basic diet was parched corn. His ministerial salary, since there was a limited money supply on the frontier, consisted of payment in old clothes or, often, "hog and hominy" at a fellow believer's homestead.

From Settlement Until the Outbreak of the Civil War

Two interesting stories about the couple have been passed down through history, the first dealing with the preacher and Dr. Charles Wright and the second with Mrs. Boleyjack and the railroad.

On one occasion, Dr. Wright was on horseback in a desolate wooded area when he heard what sounded like someone chopping down a tree. Heading the horse in the direction of the sound, the doctor came upon a physically powerful woodsman hewing a white oak log into a railroad tie. The woodsman was dressed just as described above in the typical clothing of the frontier—barefoot, deerskin trousers, a shirt and a coonskin cap—but with an additional long, woolen scarf wrapped abound both head and jaws.

The prairieland physician was able to approach the woodcutter without the latter realizing it, but not for long. Gazing at the man on horseback, the woodcutter recognized the stranger as the doctor who had recently moved into the area. After confirming that the assessment was true, the barefoot man began a conversation. According to a biographical sketch written by the doctor's son, the woodsman asked: "Do you reckon you could jerk out a bad tooth for me?" With that question began a banter back and forth between the two men until, finally, after many loud groans from the patient, the tooth was out.

Then came an awkward silence as the physician waited for the patient to ask what the charge for the procedure was. Finally, the extractor of the tooth indicated that there was need to take care of the small bill. "Pay the bill?" was the frontiersman's response.

The twenty-five-cent charge was too much, declared the man whose tooth had been removed. After a lengthy period of bargaining, the two arrived at an agreement. Dr. Wright decided on a reasonable barter: "Now, Boleyjack, if you are a preacher, just climb up on that tree stump and give me a twenty-five-cent sermon."

The backwoods preacher jumped upon a stump, decided on a text and began to preach. His sermon content focused on denouncing all people who offend those who are servants of God. The good doctor sat on his horse only a few minutes to listen to the exhortations from Boleyjack and then rode away, leaving the preacher whose voice thundered through the woodland.

Boleyjack's wife was very much like her husband. A nineteenth-century historian described her like this: "She was not too much civilized; was coarse, rough, of great physical strength and endurance. Her unadorned beauties had been materially aggravated by a savage hook in one eye, by a furious cow," which, while it had not destroyed the eye, left it permanently injured. One incident tells a lot about his character. Shortly before her death, a

Above: First Christian Church, Effingham, although established in 1867, constructed its first building in 1890.

Left: The first building of Effingham's First Baptist Church. *From* Fiftieth Anniversary Souvenir of Effingham, Illinois, *1903*.

From Settlement Until the Outbreak of the Civil War

railroad train killed her cow. The old lady witnessed it all from her cabin door. She rushed out, took her position on the track and demanded payment for her cow before the train could move. It was only after much trouble and some force that she could be gotten out of the way and the train allowed to pursue its voyage. Thereafter, she regularly soaped the track until an agent was sent down to pay a good price to the old lady for her cow.

Other frontier clergymen were traveling ministers who preached almost every day in any available spot—private homes, barrooms, barns and under trees. Camp meetings started in 1830. Itinerant preachers frequently focused their sermons on wicked lifestyles and confronted the frontiersmen with simple alternatives such as doubt or faith, sin or righteousness, hell or heaven.

Several religious meeting places had been established during the mid- to late 1830s and early 1840s. Worshipers built simple log structures, used already existing log school buildings or met in other public buildings, such as the courthouses in Ewington and, later on, Effingham. Methodist circuit riders visited their churches once a month, encouraging lay preachers to conduct services in their absence.

All of the major denominations were well represented in Effingham County during the first generation of settlement. By 1880, the Methodists

Cornerstone of the Roman Catholic church, Bishop Creek community.

Blue Point Lutheran Church, Moccasin Township.

From Settlement Until the Outbreak of the Civil War

Above: Blue Point Lutheran Church cornerstone.

Right: An early cemetery established by the community of faith, Winterrowd Christian Church.

had established congregations in twelve of the fifteen townships. Altogether, there were twenty-three congregations, including three Methodist Episcopal Church South groups. By that same year, Lutherans had established eleven congregations in eight townships, while Roman Catholics had developed nine parishes in seven townships and Baptists had established seven congregations in six townships. The same number of local governmental units saw six congregations of Christian churches and/or Churches of Christ. History books indicate Presbyterian churches only in two townships with two separate congregations. There were also two United Brethren churches in two townships and one Universalist church.

Once congregations were established, congregants were disciplined for gambling, drinking, fighting, gossiping, lying, stealing, having immoral sexual relations and horse racing. Any potential threat to the frontier's social fabric became the subject of a sermon hoping to establish a moral code that "permitted civilization to advance without invoking government restraints."

PART 3

THE CIVIL WAR AND EFFINGHAM COUNTY

The era just beyond the time of early settlement was one that left reminders etched on stone monuments, written in small diaries and painted on artist canvas. It was a time of dramatic change within the county; change that brought a deep sense of excitement as well as devastating pain. Transportation's role in the county was dramatically affected by the railroads that passed through the tall prairie grasses and led to an even greater feeling that the area was truly a crossroads for the state, indeed for all of America. There was a new energy in the air, but there was also an awareness of the great division that was tearing the nation apart.

By 1855, surveyors for the Illinois Central Railroad were in the area laying the groundwork for the construction of the Chicago to Cairo branch of the historically famous line that would carry both freight and passengers in huge numbers through seemingly endless decades. Six years before the American Civil War began, the first freight train whistled through the county; the next year witnessed the first passenger traveling the rails. The mechanical "Iron Horses" were part of the first "land grant" railroad in the United States of America.

Economically, the building of the railroad was of great importance. At the point where the rails crossed the first federal highway, a center of commerce was certain to develop. Unfortunately for Ewington, the point of crossing was two and a half miles east of the first county seat. Those who had settled in the hamlet by the Little Wabash soon got the urge to resettle nearer to what, in 1859, would become the new, and permanent, county seat at the small village of Effingham. In later years, more steam locomotives

Monument near Mason dedicated to Roswell Mason, chief engineer for the Illinois Central Railroad and mayor of Chicago during the Great Chicago Fire.

passed through the same center of government as the Terre Haute, Vandalia and St. Louis Railroad was constructed parallel to the National Road. There was also the "High and Dry," a narrow-gauge branch of the Illinois Central, a line that allowed commercial ties between Effingham and southern Indiana. The Wabash Railroad linked communities in the county—Effingham, Shumway and Altamont— as it carried people and freight north and west from the area. Effingham County's center of government housed coal bins for the trains, roundhouses and coal supplies. The railroads, so vital to the local economy, were a major source of a sense of excitement that characterized the county during the Civil War era.

There was another source of energy three miles away from the crossing of National Road and the Illinois Central tracks: the thriving German immigrant community aptly named "Teutopolis," city of the Teutons. By the end of the 1850s, there was a grand scheme coming to fruition via the plans of the Roman Catholic hierarchy living nearly one hundred miles west. The bishop at Alton, the Right Reverend Damian Juncker, had a dream of increasing the number of priests in his diocese. In 1858, he saw a way to accomplish his goal when the Franciscans arrived at Teutopolis. When Bishop Juncker approached Reverend Hennewig, pastor at Teutopolis, to get his views on the possibility of establishing a college in the Effingham County community, he was "met with a hearty response; for the latter was very desirous of offering to the boys and young men of his parish and of the surrounding territory an opportunity to obtain a higher education. The

The Civil War and Effingham County

matter was thoroughly discussed and, as there could be no question of two institutions, it was decided that the projected institution should serve both as a high school and as the diocesan seminary."

The local priest, full of energy and bursting with enthusiasm, immediately began the process needed to complete the project. First, at a meeting of parishioners on October 9, 1860, a committee was set in place to both select the site for the school and to begin gathering money needed for construction. The "Program" document drawn up on that October day stated:

Portion of the monument for Teutopolis's St. Joseph's Monastery.

> *Since the town of Teutopolis, on account of its healthful climate and retired location, appears to afford a suitable site for an institution of learning; and since the Rt. Rev. Bishop Damian H. Juncker desires to possess in his diocese a Seminary, equipped according to the canonical regulations, in which pious and gifted young men who feel called to the priesthood can be properly trained for the holy ministry, for the honor of God, their own salvation, and that of their fellowmen; and since his Lordship has graciously accepted the offer of the town to erect a seminary building, with the assurance that, if the local and the surrounding parishes successfully carry out this undertaking, they, as the first, should exclusively possess an institution of this kind,… the inhabitants of this town and of the surrounding territory have agreed to contribute, according to their means, toward this useful purpose…Thus done at Teutopolis, on October 19, 1860, with the approbation of the Superiors, as testifies the President of the Building Committee,*
> *DAMIAN HENNEWIG, Praeses.*

The spring of 1861, the year the American Civil War began, witnessed the start of construction of the school. Work moved rapidly, so much so that on July 2, Father Damian, in the name of the bishop, was able to solemnly bless the cornerstone of the new building. By Christmas, the Teutopolis priest was able to declare:

> *Our Seminary building is finished to the roof, by dint of the greatest exertion and amid prospects far from promising. If I had not pushed the work with all my might, we should not have got beyond the foundation walls, and the congregation would perhaps have lost confidence in the undertaking. The building now stands a stately structure and, they say, an ornament to Teutopolis, 80 feet long by 50 feet wide, a four-story building, offering accommodations for 50–80 students. All now depends on the support we find; in case we find support, we shall, with the help of God, continue the work this coming year until it is completed.*

Full view of the St. Joseph's Monastery monument.

The Civil War and Effingham County

But there was war, a secular event that had consequences for the religious realm. On February 10, 1862, Father Damian wrote:

> *The Seminary building is now under roof, but the treasury, owing to these sad war times, is exhausted, so that, unless we obtain aid from elsewhere, we are at a loss how to continue. I was appointed president of the Building Committee by the Bishop, and in consequence have had many cares and anxieties. To be able to continue building operations, I saw myself compelled to go to Cincinnati. I have just returned from that city.*

It would have been easy to lose hope, but for words of encouragement, such as the thoughts of Father Herbert, who was to become the first rector of the college:

> *Ever since, all eyes in the diocese are directed to Teutopolis, yes, even Missouri is interested; for, as the Rt. Rev. Joseph Melcher, Vicar-General, and other priests say, his Grace, the Archbishop of St. Louis, will undoubtedly send hither his seminarians, as soon as the institution is ready to receive them. The Bishop will probably send the seminarians who are now studying at other institutions in this country or abroad, because, as he says, he is not able to meet the expenses which their education elsewhere entails.*

By August 1862, the structure was finished and ready to occupy. On Sunday, September 15, the solemn dedication took place. At seven o'clock, Father Nazarius Kommerscheid, who had been ordained by Bishop Juncker in the parish church the day before, said his first Holy Mass, in the presence of the bishop. When the services concluded, a procession consisting of the students, seminarians, community of the friary, invited guests and officiating clergy marched to the new building for ceremonies, which included English and German addresses emphasizing the importance of the institution for the diocese, praising the zeal of the Franciscans and of the people and expressing the heartiest good wishes for a successful future.

On the next day, September 16, the first scholastic year began with only six seminarians and twenty-five high school students. By the end of the school year, those numbers had increased to eight and fifty, respectively. Thirty of the non-seminarians were residents of Effingham County. During the second school year, 1863–64, there were eleven seminarians and fifty-two students in the high school department; during the following year, the seminarians numbered sixteen, while forty-eight students pursued the high school course. Most of the latter came from towns in Illinois; several are recorded, during these first years, as being from Missouri; while there was one each from Ohio, New York and Louisiana. Hopes were high that the college would continue to expand with each passing year.

The community of faith at Teutopolis was the focus of other religious activity during the Civil War era, the most significant of which was the arrival of a saintly visitor from Aachen, a city in the mother country of the village's residents.

> *At midnight we started for Teutopolis, where we have a branch house. Bishop Juncker, whom I had met at Munich, had persistently urged its foundation. We rode in the railroad cars till five in the evening and then a two hours' journey in a rattling cart over a non-descript road was yet before us. One of our drivers called out: "Hold on fast, so as not to fall out. Here is a bad place. Last year one of my boys fell out here and broke his arm." We Sisters, and two other passengers, each sat on a chair. But finally, I preferred to take my place on the bottom of our vehicle, because the chairs were jostled about so roughly. At seven in the evening we arrived at Teutopolis.*

So wrote Mother Frances Schervier in July 1863 during the middle of the American Civil War. Her visit was part of a special journey to visit America because, as her biographer wrote, she "yearned to see her children in America, and to observe how they prospered in their vocation under conditions totally different from those in Europe." The "children" to whom she referred were the sisters who were part of a small colony of the Sisters of the Poor of St. Francis, a congregation founded by Mother Frances in 1845.

Within five years, the small colony of sisters in America had experienced rapid growth. There were two houses in Mrs. Peter's home city, as well as houses in new locations such as New York City, New York; Columbus, Ohio; Teutopolis, Illinois; and Hoboken, New Jersey.

Mother Frances's letters are interesting for the insights they give into her life, but they also offer insight into what other migrants experienced as they traveled across the ocean and into interior America. Particularly, people with ancestors who traveled from Germany during the mid-nineteenth century can gain an understanding of what their ancestors had to endure as they traveled to their new homes in Effingham County.

She wrote about seasickness, violent storms on the ocean and "coffin-like" beds in a gloomy little space on the ship; but she also wrote about

The Civil War and Effingham County

times of joy and of great hope. She reflected on the role of faith in her life. These were certainly typical of many experiences of Europeans who came to America in the mid- to late nineteenth century.

After a brief stay on the East Coast, Mother Frances and a companion nun traveled into the interior of the United States: first to Ohio, then to Indiana and finally to Illinois. Each stage of the journey brought with it great fatigue, a state of exhaustion. While at Fort Wayne, Indiana, Mother Frances set in motion the process necessary to found another house. She wrote that she and the sister had traveled nine hours by rail and then two more hours in a country wagon. Her description of the rural roads was that they were so bad that "we continually invoked our guardian angel." After returning to Fort Wayne the next day, by midnight of the same day, the trip to Teutopolis began. More heartache awaited the devout travelers. On July 6, 1863, Mother Frances wrote:

> *A novice, Sister Xaveria, was dangerously ill with typhoid fever. She has anxiously yearned for my presence. After saluting Our Saviour in the chapel, I went to her.*
>
> *Though she was delirious she left her bed when I entered, fell on her knees and regarded me with an angelic expression. Her folded hands indicated that she implored my blessing. I was moved to tears. She soon became unconscious. The bishop had the kindness to visit the dying sister in the morning. He said three Our Fathers with us, and then went to give confirmation in church. He also sang High Mass and preached. I remained with the sick sister, who rendered her dear soul to God with visible agony about eleven o'clock the same morning. From the beginning of her illness she had a presentiment that she would die, and had willing offered her young life to God.*

The sisters' stay in Teutopolis was only from July 4 until July 7. Cincinnati was the next location on the itinerary. They were bothered by the humid weather, but most of all, they were troubled by the terror of the American Civil War. On July 15, Mother Frances wrote to a sister:

> *You would not feel at home here on account of the tremendous war clamor. The stores are closed; the men are drilling and shooting all day long. The enemy's troops are manoeuvering within fifty to sixty miles of the city, and some time ago had advanced even closer, when the archbishop requested the prayers of our recluses. They try to comply with great earnestness, in which*

I confirmed them. And the good, pious archbishop ascribes it to their prayers that the city was spared. We have not the least fear. So reckless a spirit predominates here, that one makes light of everything.

Two days later, she penned: "Great excitement and ceaseless drumming in the city. The enemy is approaching. Here and there the railroads are torn up, and connections are impossible. When, a few days ago, a thick cloud of dust arose, the enemy was thought to be advancing. Anxiety turned into general merriment, when the cause of the dust became known: a large drove of mules were driven to Cincinnati to be employed in the war."

The saintly woman's compassion was stirred when she visited the hospitals: "I visited all the sick in the great hospital. Most of them are Germans. I was greatly delighted to be able to speak to them. Oh, how necessary the exercise of charity is in this country! One must have experienced it to believe it. Here is the place to aid the poor souls by corporal words of mercy."

What she was experiencing, of course, was also what the people of Effingham County came to know firsthand.

It was in April 1861 when President Lincoln issued his call: "WHEREAS, The laws of the United States have been and are opposed in several States by combinations too powerful to be suppressed in the ordinary way, I therefore call for the militia of the several States of the Union, to the aggregate number of 75,000, to suppress said combination and execute the laws." Lincoln went on to set quotas that every state had to contribute to the total war effort in terms of soldiers. Governors had to decide how to respond. Illinois's response was described in a news release in *Harper's Weekly* on April 27, 1861:

> *Illinois Governor Yates has issued a proclamation to convene the Legislature of his State at Springfield on the 23d April, for the purpose of enacting such laws and adopting such measures as may be deemed necessary upon the following subject, to wit: The more perfect organization and equipment of the militia of the State, and placing the same upon the best footing to render efficient assistance to the General Government in preserving the Union, enforcing the laws, protecting the property and rights of the people, and also the raising of such money and other means as may be required to carry out the foregoing objects. The troops are mustering, and ready to go forward.*

The process for the state was simple. First, the quota was enumerated for each county and then for each township. The message was sent out to

The Civil War and Effingham County

the county seats. Effingham County received the plea via the telegraph. S.A. Newcomb, Illinois Central agent, was the telegrapher who received the message and then posted it in the new county seat, the tiny hamlet of Effingham.

Nearly every aspect of life changed as a result of the war. The county experienced a lot of economic change, and, of course, there were red-hot discussions focusing on political matters. Of far greater importance, however, was what happened economically. For example, Effingham County's transportation system, so vital to prosperity, was put on hold as the chartering of the Vandalia and Terre Haute Railroad was deferred to a post–Civil War time. The main concern for the state was the development of north–south rail routes so that both soldiers and supplies could get to the locations related to the war effort. That seemed to slow down economic growth locally.

There was general farm prosperity in this county, however. Farmers saw the following dramatic changes in prices paid for produce and livestock: wheat went from $0.85 per bushel to $1.75, and corn went from $0.25 to $1.05. Similar increases in livestock prices were evident, as cattle went from $2.25 to $8.00; hog prices increased by 300 percent. It was a time of economic boom.

The war also spurred social change. There was a great loss of manpower through near depopulation of the males of the county as the young and able-bodied went to war. That brought significant changes: some agricultural matters simply came to an end, while other matters adjusted to the times. The Effingham County Agricultural Society ceased after the annual fair in 1861 because the secretary, Sam Moffitt, went to war. Many county women experienced a changing role as their work expanded to include much more direct involvement in the farm fields. Some women even volunteered to be nurses on the battlefields so they could tend to their loved ones and make sure they returned after the war was over. One was Martha Abraham from Watson, a woman who went to Murfreesboro, Tennessee, to care for her son after he was wounded at Stones River. Unfortunately, while there, she took sick and died.

Because the war did not end, the military draft came into existence. Once again, there were quotas for the county that, in turn, led to quotas for each township. For the most part, Effingham County had a limited need for a draft due to large numbers of volunteers.

All males in the county were placed in one of two classes: first class— composed of all men liable to military service between the ages of twenty and thirty-five—and second class—all unmarried men fit for duty above the age of thirty-five but below forty-five.

Bounties were used to encourage volunteers. The County Board of Supervisors made donations totaling $27,500 from the county treasury to support the system.

The draft led to some new issues involving county residents. Because draftees could hire replacements, a new business enterprise developed organized by men who were dealers in substitutes. Sometimes Democrats complained that there seemed to be a lot of politics involved in determining who was selected for conscription. Once chosen, there was limited local training for the draftees. The most prominent location for introducing the men to the nature of military life was the open field in front of the Broom Trading Post on the Shelbyville-Salem Road.

Potential soldiers were not the only ones whose daily lives were affected by the war; change was in the air for all citizens. Even children's games frequently consisted of forming play battalions, making breastworks and clay forts and having triumphal marches when news of a Union victory arrived in town. Public discussions focused on matters such as troop movements, presidential orders and Horace Greeley's editorials. There was a hunger for knowing about what was taking place.

Effingham County also experienced rapid population growth. The fact that many refugees from Civil War battle areas moved to this area during the rebellion brought various concerns. One was the fear that these new residents from the South would sabotage the war effort; another was that schools could not keep up with the influx of students. Watson School in 1864, for example, had 101 students taught by Mary T. Hillis, a young first-year teacher.

Chief among the social change, however, was the way in which the County's 7,800 citizens interacted. Racially, the area was nearly all white, with only 11 people of color having residence in the county. In terms of gender, there were 575 more males than females. The citizenry came from a variety of countries and a variety of states. This was very significant for the Civil War era because it called into question what role each group would have in the time period that so deeply divided the United States.

Of the 982 foreign-born residents, 900 were individuals whose native tongue either was not English or whose English was spoken with a thick accent: more than 700 of them spoke German; over 100 were Irish; 16 spoke French; 15 were Scottish; and 10 spoke Danish. Added to the mix were small numbers of Norwegians, Swedes, Austrians and Swiss, along with at least 1 each from Wales, Mexico, Italy, Holland and Finland.

The Civil War and Effingham County

Union loyalists wanted to know whether these immigrants had allegiance to the country and its preservation. Could they be counted on to help with the war effort?

More troubling was the great number of Effingham Country residents who had been born in slaveholding states. There were about 100 fewer in this category than found listed among the foreign-born. They came from Tennessee (288), Kentucky (276), Virginia (167), North Carolina (91), Missouri (23), Alabama (18), South Carolina (8), Arkansas (5), Texas (5), Mississippi (3), Georgia (2) and Louisiana (2). For these citizens, the basic question was: "What side would they be on?" Many people in this part of Illinois and southward had a strong secessionist viewpoint.

Of great significance was the political party loyalty of the residents. Throughout Illinois in the election of 1860, only 51 percent of the voters had supported the Republican Abraham Lincoln. Some feared that Democrats would not be loyal to the Union. All townships except Lucas were Democratic. In fact, Lucas Township, the only Republican township, in 1863 had only one Democratic vote. In the 1860 presidential election, the Effingham County results were 65 to 70 percent voting for Democratic candidate Stephen A. Douglas. That situation remained true after the war as well, when in 1868, there were 3,201 votes for Democratic candidate Horatio Seymour but only 209 votes for Ulysses S. Grant, the Republican standard-bearer. Many wondered if a Democratic county would provide soldiers for the national cause. The final results were astonishing. The 1860 census showed Effingham County had approximately two thousand males between the ages of fifteen and forty-six. When looking at the total number of soldiers who served from the county, the number is nearly the same. The support for the Union was widespread. Effingham County showed its loyalty. Virtually every major battlefield had people from Effingham County fighting and dying to hold the Union together.

Patriotism was extremely strong. In the community of Mason, a flag was raised with the message, "Death to traitors," a warning intended to intimidate those who may have been thinking about not supporting the war. In the city of Effingham, there was a meeting on the courthouse lawn that organized a local unit of volunteers and gathered money to send them on their way to Springfield to be formally enrolled in military service.

German patriotism was very antislavery in nature. Upon presentation of quotas in the Teutopolis area, there was a tremendously positive response. Just as in many other parts of the United States, Effingham County witnessed the intense participation of the German population in the war effort. Life, both at home and on the battlefield, was to change radically.

Effingham County

In reminiscing about the war, Dr. James Newton Matthews wrote about conditions in his hometown:

> [In] *a few days a company of the Eleventh Illinois Infantry, three months' volunteers, left Mason for the tented field. And still the excitement waxed higher. Every train that thundered southward was loaded down with boys in blue and huge engines of war. Companies of home guards and minute men were formed, and paraded the streets almost daily in their battle-robes, awaiting anxiously their marching orders.*
>
> *Such were the scenes that Mason presented in the terrible spring and summer of 1861. The cry was "Liberty and Union," and he was but a traitor or a craven who refused to raise his hand in defense of his falling country at that time. When the spring of 1862 dawned there were only one or two young men left in the town above the age of sixteen. The rest had wandered off to the war—some to fall in battle, others to perish in Southern prisons.*

Matthews's words could have described almost every part of the county. Soon, sad news began to become part of routine conversation. Many of those who left for service to their country were not going to return alive. Andrew J. Allen, Company G of the Eleventh Illinois, came home to Ewington Cemetery as the result of dying in camp at Bird's Point, Missouri, during a measles epidemic. In the spring of the next year, his brother, William, was placed at his side. Mortally wounded at Fort Donelson, the second brother was returned to Illinois, only to die at Mound City. Grief was widespread.

Colonel T.E.G Ransom, resident of Farina, much wounded hero of the Eleventh Illinois Infantry.

Many soldiers from the area went into battle and sent back

The Civil War and Effingham County

General W.H.L. Wallace, beloved commander of the Eleventh Illinois Infantry, killed at Shiloh.

Ewington cemetery marker indicating graves of two brothers who died early in the Civil War.

One of many Civil War veterans' gravestones in Ewington Cemetery.

letters or were the subjects of newspaper correspondents' reports. Local residents learned about war and battle from soldiers such as one who wrote about Fort Donelson:

> *The battle was fought in dense timber, on very high hills and deep ravines, and nearly the whole of the fighting was done by the enemy outside of their entrenchments. The lines of the battle extended over a space of three or four miles, and the whole distance is thickly strewn with the pits of the dead. I noticed one trench containing 61 bodies of the Eleventh Illinois, and alongside of it a trench of rebel dead of about the same length, but I had no means of ascertaining how many were in it. Each company generally buried its own dead together, and marked the name of each one on a shingle stuck down at his head.*

Another enlistee, Henry Uptmor, described seeing his first dead soldier—a fellow Teutopolis citizen:

> *The very first corpse I came upon was that of my sleeping companion, George Gerhard Weis, the stouthearted God fearing youth. He was lying*

The Civil War and Effingham County

Effingham County resident Lucius Rose, captain of Company G, Eleventh Illinois Infantry.

> *with his face turned upward, looking toward Heaven, with his arms outstretched as if he wished to say, "Dear Father in Heaven, take me up to you in your Kingdom, for I am tired of this life on earth." May the Lord grant him eternal rest! The bullet had pierced his lower lip, and came out through the nape of the neck to carry on and on its speed. Soon I found another comrade, another good young fellow named Karl Zerrusen. He was well covered and I found his body still warm, a sign that he had died only a short time before I came upon him. He had been wounded in the abdomen and must have suffered much pain before he passed away. May the Lord grant him eternal rest! Then I walked around the battlefield to meditate upon it, and I found many other wounded.*

One soldier said the bullets were like a heavy snowstorm. Many from Effingham died or were wounded at the Tennessee fort.

A newspaper reporter wrote:

> *Among the wounded on that glorious field day was Capt. L.M. Rose, Company G, Eleventh Illinois, whose name has not before been reported. He was formerly the editor of the Effingham (Ill.) Gazette. He received*

Grand Army of the Republic monument in Effingham's Oak Ridge Cemetery.

four wounds by bullets; one in each hip, in the left shoulder, and left hand… Capt. Rose and Major Chipman, of the 2nd Iowa…laid two days in the woods before they were discovered, and the first night upon the ground in a drenching rain storm, suffering inconceivable pain.

Across five Aprils, from 1861 until 1865, the harsh reality of war came home via the mail and the newspaper. There was much pain and sadness in a nation that was deeply divided. Even the major religious denominations were divided. There was, for instance, a Methodist Episcopal Church, South, a group that supported a states' rights viewpoint, which was a political stance most entrenched in the Deep South. Several such congregations exited in Effingham County.

In some ways, the area was a microcosm of the United States, especially when it came to the strong feelings people had about the war. Those who supported the Union cause were full of patriotic fervor. In Mason, Goddard's Hotel became a focal point for rallies. Pro-Union meetings also were held at

The Civil War and Effingham County

the Mason Baptist Church. In part due to the great number of enlistments from the community and its immediately surrounding area, Teutopolis Township came into existence.

There were Effingham County residents with strong antislavery sentiments. One such person was H.H. Wright, who wrote about his family's experiences. He described his father's acquaintanceship with the famous abolitionist leader Elijah Lovejoy:

> *At that date* [1827] *the boat crossed the river twice a day and there were 20,000 inhabitants in the city. My Father stayed there that summer and worked at his trade. He got good wages while there, but there was a feeling on the slavery question and Lovejoy was printing a Free Soil Paper and my Father being raised a Quaker He read his paper and a friend of Lovejoy's and I recollect Lovejoy well when he was ordered to leave St. Louis. His friends thought it not safe and left also. Lovejoy went to Alton and was killed. His horse threw in the river.*

The great moral debate about the issue of slavery and the need to support President Lincoln as he tried to keep the country united as a single nation gave rise to a network of pro-Union newspapers in this part of the state. The *Loyalist* was an Effingham County newspaper printed in Mason with George Brewster as editor and publisher. He was described by those who knew him as a talented and educated man who, although not a firebrand in personality, could create strong emotional responses in people by what he wrote. For nearly nine months, beginning in April 1863, his seven-column folio became a "Red-hot exponent of abolitionism." With the motto of "Union and Liberty, Now and Forever, One and Inseparable," the newspaper located in the village of two hundred people printed scorching editorials berating deserters and local insurgents. Of course, there were war news, stories describing what was significant in the strategy for winning the war, soldiers' letters and heartfelt defenses of the president. Correspondents, such as J.N. Matthews and others, went to the newspaper office carrying weapons due to the frequent threats of violence. The *Loyalist* building became the gathering place for Unionists who came together to conduct political rallies.

A large number of "Peace Democrats" showed the other side of the divided citizenry. Toward the end of May 1861, the *Chicago Tribune* carried an article in which an individual spoke of hearing a portion of a letter that the very prominent William Yancey, a proslavery extremist, had written to a citizen of Effingham County rejoicing in the fact that the North was full of people who were sworn to the insurrection cause, that there were "Golden Circles" of Southern supporters to be found throughout the Union. These secret "Copperhead" societies were a real presence in the central and southern parts of Illinois.

In the abolitionist newspaper the *Centralia Sentinel*, a correspondent wrote:

> *A somewhat extended visit to the counties of Coles, Jasper, Edgar, Clark, Effingham, Moultrie, Christian and Montgomery,…has not only satisfied me that the reported strength of the order in Illinois was not exaggerated, but that in many of the counties above enumerated, whole communities are ripe for rebellion…In Clark and Effingham counties there are no soldiers, and treason flourisheth in consequence.*

The "Peace Democrats" were involved in many activities. Near Mason, there were those citizens who denounced the president, Northern soldiers, Loyalist citizens and, of course, the war. Through their words and deeds, they tried to intimidate the opposition forces. These Copperheads planned one or two futile attempts to lay the town in ashes. They wore distinctive "Butternut badges" that pictured "Lady Liberty" carrying a national flag like a rag in her hand. The threat posed by such antiwar forces within Effingham County led to formation of the Union League to counteract any hostile activities that the "Peace Democrats" might carry out.

To many individuals, Effingham County seemed like rebel territory. In fact, that attitude was reflected by the well-known Civil War nurse Mary

"Mother" Newcomb, volunteer nurse after burying her soldier husband in Effingham. *From* Four Years of Personal Reminiscences of the War, *1893.*

The Civil War and Effingham County

Newcomb. She told about her experiences with the war's opponents in the tiny village that was the county seat when she wrote:

> *We arrived at Effingham, the home of my son, at noon Wednesday, only to find that he had enlisted in the Twenty-sixth Illinois Infantry, and was already gone; but his wife was at home to receive us. My husband grew worse rapidly, and at eleven o'clock on Thursday evening he died—just nine days after he was wounded. The last word he said was: "Mary, go back and take care of the boys, they need you." Alone among strangers, in a rebel community, and my only son gone to the army, I felt very lonely. Mothers know that an only son means much, especially when one has laid a husband upon the country's altar. It seemed more than I could bear. My son was then in Missouri, near Cairo. He was telegraphed for, but army regulations would not permit him to come.*
>
> *On the 2nd of March, 1862, they laid away my loved one. At that time there was a strong rebel sentiment prevailing in Effingham county, and it was said I could not get a loyal minister to officiate at the funeral. I said I would have a loyal one or none at all. Mr. Newcomb was a strong Presbyterian, but there was no Presbyterian minister to be had. A Methodist minister sent me word that he would take the risk, and I gladly accepted his offer. There was a great danger of a riot at the funeral, for the court house*

Window dedicated to Mary Newcomb at the former Effingham First Presbyterian Church.

was the only place that would hold the people, and some of the rebels said we should not use it; but I found a few loyal friends who stood by me, and we laid my loved one in his grave—the second soldier buried in the cemetery.

The experiences of Reverend Alfred Bliss, who moved to Effingham in the 1880s and the man for whom Effingham's Bliss Park was named, validated Mary Newcomb's claims. As was the case with many Methodist clergymen, Bliss had a reputation for taking a strong stand against slavery. That stand nearly cost him his life on more than one occasion. He became a pistol-packing preacher due to the serious threat posed by supporters of a desperado named Thomas Clingman, a man who had a reputation of being an officer in the Confederate army. His force of upward of one thousand guerilla soldiers wreaked havoc near the Bliss farm in Montgomery County, not too far from Vandalia. At night, a hired man and one of the preacher's sons stood watch to be sure that Clingman's raiders did not destroy farm buildings.

A favorite tool of the Copperheads was the torch. Rumors were widespread that several area Methodist church buildings and some schools were set afire by the pro-Southern sympathizers. In the immediate aftermath of the Civil War, the *Centralia Sentinel* carried an article about "the torches of Effingham secesh." The writer told about the need to destroy the torches that Effingham County Copperheads had planned to use to burn houses of abolitionist leaders in Salem. When the Eccles school near Beecher City burned in 1863, Copperheads were suspected of arson since both the Golden Circle Democrats and the Union League Republicans held meetings at the facility.

More evidence of the great divide came in early September 1863, when a detachment of the Sixteenth Illinois Cavalry led by a Captain Jackson attempted to arrest some deserters near Mason. About twenty other citizens came to the aid of those being arrested. Shots were exchanged, during which two cavalrymen were wounded, as were five deserters and several of their supporters. The county was greatly agitated by this event. The public clearly was polarized, yet daily life continued, and when the war came to an end in 1865, those divisions were put to one side as the citizens worked to restore the goodwill that had marked the area before the great struggle had begun.

But for many of Effingham County's citizens, the reminders and remembrances of the tragic war would make a mark lasting for a lifetime. For families who had lost loved ones, there was the knowledge that sons often had been buried hundreds of miles away from home in places where it was highly unlikely that family members would ever visit the grave site. For others, there were the white gravestones marking the final resting place in local cemeteries. And for still others, those for whose sons there was no accounting, there was no finality to the war.

There were lasting emotional feelings for many of the soldiers. Especially devastating were the memories that many experienced in the infamous Andersonville Prison Camp. The Dieterich area's John W. Richards, of the Ninety-eighth Mounted Infantry, told about the horrifying conditions from which he and two other soldiers escaped. Another Effingham County soldier, Joseph Bohn, suffered through the dirty, filthy conditions and malignant ulcers that covered the entire length of his back, leaving scars that he carried to his grave when he died in 1918. Robert Gibson, a member of the Thirty-eighth Illinois Infantry and Mason resident, left for war a strong, healthy young man but returned from Andersonville emaciated as the result of the barbarous conditions he lived through. Others from the county experienced the same.

Some of the most detailed memories were set forth in a book by volunteer nurse Mary Newcomb. When the Civil War broke out, Mary was visiting her family, so when her husband enlisted in the Eleventh Illinois Infantry she came home to an empty dwelling. Because she grew lonesome, she decided to travel to where her husband was—Birds Point, Missouri.

Almost immediately, she became an active part of army life. A black measles epidemic, called such because the victims turned black after dying, had stricken the camp. There was a dramatic need for a nurse. Although technically she was not supposed to serve in that capacity, Mary immediately began her work, ably assisted by a teenager from Effingham County who was assigned to her. She was only briefly away from the army on a couple of occasions because she grew so attached to the Eleventh Illinois.

She was only in her mid-forties, but she became "Mother" to the unit. She did many things. She helped in times of crisis. She consoled when disaster struck. She wrote letters for the soldiers. She accompanied bodies of the deceased to their home communities. She witnessed the great pain and agony suffered by soldiers during the American Civil War. She knew that many of the young men were quite fearful about what would happen to them. She especially saw the fear when the soldiers faced amputation of limbs. She became their advocate and nurse, arguing their case before the doctors. She was nearby when the men fought in the major battles of Fort Donelson and Shiloh. She was there aboard the hospital ships helping the soldiers who survived. She was there working with poor whites and former slaves whose lives had been displaced by the war. She knew war up close, and she knew the pain.

After the war was over, in Effingham she and her daughter-in-law became quite involved in business activities, leading her to remain an active part

Above left: The Newcomb family gravestone at Oak Ridge Cemetery, Effingham.

Above right: Women's Relief Corps, adjunct to the GAR monument, Oak Ridge Cemetery, Effingham.

of the community until her death during the Christmas season in 1892. Because of the great respect they had for her, members of the Grand Army of the Republic gave her a funeral with their rites, an unusual circumstance for that group.

Although there were many negative aspects of the war, there was also a positive side to the conflict that tore the nation apart. The war produced leaders, individuals who became deeply involved in the life of the communities within the county. One of the great examples of such a person was Benson Wood, a Union army officer during the American Civil War.

Originally from Pennsylvania and then a teacher and principal at Franklin Grove Academy in Lee County, Illinois, when the Civil War broke out, Wood's

The Civil War and Effingham County

life dramatically changed. As a first lieutenant, Company C, the "Rock River Rifles," Thirty-fourth Regiment, Illinois Volunteer Infantry, Wood's horse was shot from under him during the bloody battle of Shiloh, but he was not wounded. Due to brave and efficient service during the battle, the young soldier was promoted to the rank of captain on October 6, 1862.

Wood was involved in the siege and battle at Corinth and in the Battle of Stone's River. But the war took its toll on him, undermining his health, so the young officer resigned his position and was officially discharged on January 29, 1863.

Women's Relief Corps monument of the Effingham County Courthouse square.

From the terrors of war, Benson Wood entered the University of Chicago, where he studied law, graduating on June 8, 1864, as the valedictorian of his class. By July 6 of the same year, the ex–Civil War soldier was admitted to the bar, being licensed by the Illinois Supreme Court to practice law in all the courts of the state. Shortly thereafter, he traveled to Effingham, a town in its infancy, to set up a law practice by joining a partnership.

Effingham County's deep involvement in the politics of the day appealed to Attorney Wood. He enjoyed public debate about national and local elections, as well as the huge political rallies in the county seat in the weeks and days before the election. Quite quickly, Wood joined the political arena.

When the Republican Party met in its state convention in Springfield in September 1870, it selected Benson Wood as a vice-president of the statewide party, representing the eleventh legislative district. Two years later, in a presidential election year, Benson Wood was a candidate of the Republican Party, running for a seat in the Illinois House of Representatives. He was victorious and became a member of the Twenty-eighth General Assembly of the state of Illinois.

During the mid- to late 1870s, Wood also was deeply involved in a flurry of activities. In September 1874, the Effingham lawyer was named as judge advocate general for the Illinois National Guard. In 1876, the Illinois Republican Convention named Benson Wood as one of the delegates to the National Convention, which was held in Cincinnati that year. In 1878, Brigadier General Benson Wood was a member of the committee called to create a new bill for militia law.

By the end of the decade, Benson Wood's name was well known throughout the state, so much so that when the Republican Party was ready to nominate Shelby M. Cullom for the gubernatorial post in 1880, Benson Wood was on the short list to be nominated as lieutenant governor. In 1880, Wood was also being given serious consideration as the congressional nominee from his district.

Although not elected to either post in the Illinois executive branch or in the federal legislative branch, Wood continued to build more of a reputation for himself as a member of the National Republican Party and as an orator, while continuing his local law practice. Finally, in 1894, Wood became the Republican nominee of the nineteenth Illinois congressional district. Although Mr. Wood had quite a good reputation and his oratorical skills served him well, William McKinley, at that time governor of Ohio and later president of the United States, traveled to Illinois to help campaign for the Effingham resident. Along with a great number of other Republicans, Wood was elected to Congress, serving one term during the second administration of Grover Cleveland. As one of the victorious candidates, the Effingham man was a chief speaker at a "monster jollification meeting" in Vandalia that celebrated the Republican successes. Then it was off to Washington, D.C., to combat President Cleveland's policies.

The local lawyer continued to be a popular speaker at other types of rallies in the area, especially at veterans' affairs and also at the funerals of political leaders in the state. In similar fashion, Wood was among the chief members of the delegations sent to talk to the potential candidates.

By 1896, following the lead of Richland County, Effingham County was once again ready to nominate Benson Wood for Congress. Later on, other county conventions in the district did the same. This time the sentiments of the nineteenth district were decidedly more Democratic than in the previous election. Political pundits wrote that because of the "silverite" issue, the incumbent congressman was practically defeated before the election took place.

In the aftermath of his brief congressional career, Mr. Wood remained a vital part of the Illinois cultural landscape. In 1897, Governor Tanner appointed the former American Civil War officer as a trustee of the soldiers'

The Civil War and Effingham County

and orphans' home in Normal. In that same year, he also was elected as a vice-president of the Illinois State Bar Association, a group for which he eventually served as president. Benson Wood was the principal speaker of the day when President Theodore Roosevelt visited Rockford, Illinois, in 1903 to dedicate Memorial Hall. In that same year, thousands of people lined the streets of San Francisco to witness a huge parade of veterans of the Grand Army of the Republic. A newspaper reporter wrote: "Headed by a detachment from Illinois commanded by Benson Wood, the Grand Army detachments appeared in full muster at their appointed stations, ready to move with the main column which started punctually at 10 o'clock."

GAR monument, Union Cemetery, Mason.

The next year, 1904, found Wood speaking at the Illinois State Bar Association banquet. That same year, the former congressman was the chief representative of the governor of Illinois when ceremonies dedicating the Illinois monument at Shiloh battlefield took place.

In 1906, he was a participant at the Cullom Conference in Chicago; in 1907, a delegate to the Trust Conference; and in 1908, the main speaker at the dedication of the new Illinois Supreme Court building. When he died in 1915, there was an abundance of tributes for him. Benson Wood was a transitional figure from the Civil War era who, as a leader from Effingham County, helped move the area into the twentieth century.

PART 4

EFFINGHAM COUNTY DURING THE LATTER NINETEENTH CENTURY

The last three decades of the nineteenth century provided considerable change in Effingham County. The transition from a frontier-type setting to a more stable social environment reflecting prosperity began. The county built a new courthouse, the pride and joy of the whole populace. Trains brought people and products into the area. The growth of the local print media provided citizens with detailed information about their part of the country, as well as knowledge of world news. Nationally known politicians delivered orations on the courthouse steps. New buildings, including private homes, reflected a growing economy. Area residents gained national fame. A sense of transformation was in the air.

The Effingham County Courthouse was symbolic of the sense of permanence and community that characterized the post–Civil War prairie county in the Illinois heartland. The Second Empire–style building that dominates the square in Effingham was not the first edifice constructed for the county courts. In fact, there had been three before—two in Ewington, the original county seat, and one in Effingham. In less than forty years' time, from 1833 until 1871, all four structures were built

By 1869, the third courthouse of Effingham County was judged to be in an unsafe condition. Although repairs were ordered to correct the problem, before anything could be done to remedy the situation, a fire that broke out on the morning of March 17, 1869, completely razed the building.

Discussions about the construction of a new courthouse took place over several months' time at various meetings of the county board. Finally, on

Effingham County During the Latter Nineteenth Century

Steam locomotive crossing bridge over the Little Wabash River near Mason. *Courtesy of the Mason Civic Center, Mason, Illinois.*

April 15, 1870, the group agreed to build a new structure following the plans submitted by a St. Louis architect, William Brown. There were a lot of other details to be worked out, but by June 16, 1870, construction was underway. On that day, the board adopted a resolution to invite Effingham Lodge No. 149 of the AF and AM, with other lodges in the county, to perform the ceremony of laying the cornerstone on July 15. The people of the county were also invited to be in attendance, and they came in great numbers to witness an elaborate affair.

Construction continued during the rest of the year and was finished early in 1871. Immediately, the building became the focus of pride throughout the whole county. The county commissioners' records showed an "actual cost of construction was $33,226.20. Fixtures for $3,279.60 and miscellaneous items not properly belonging to courthouse construction amounting to $1,436.70 raised the total to $37,942.50."

Pride came from other sources also. The county's citizens became quite aware that they were living in "Crossroads County," where the land transportation facilities played such a major role in the economic and social history. Area residents saw the large trestles and the great number of railroad tracks connecting all parts of the county. They realized that life was changing radically.

By the early 1880s, as one historian wrote: "The people of Effingham had heard so much about railroads coming—singly, in squads and in

Steam locomotive nearing Effingham in the early twentieth century.

platoons—that they were dazed with their own prospective greatness." But when the Springfield & South-Eastern Railroad began to seek support for a route through the county, Effingham hesitated, while the townships of West, Mason and Liberty and the village of Edgewood secured the road, with Edgewood giving $10,000, West Township $10,000, Mason Township $10,000 and Liberty $5,000. The road ran through Edgewood and Altamont, twelve miles east of Effingham, on to Springfield.

The railroad history of the era shows that Effingham County during those exciting years was transitioning from a "Wild West" type of society into one reflective of Victorian lifestyles, with economic prosperity at its core. Two examples from 1875 show that the frontier spirit was still in vogue. Both of them are rooted in tragedy.

The weather mirrored the feelings of the citizens of Effingham in early July 1875 on the day of the funeral of Milo Eames, a Vandalia line engineer who had been murdered on July 8, just a few days earlier, approximately twenty-five miles from the Presbyterian church where Reverend Pollock delivered an eloquent message of consolation for the family.

The community was crowded with people who had traveled from a wide area to attend the funeral rites. From Terre Haute, Indiana, the city where Eames and his young bride had moved after being married, to Effingham, there was a train of seven or eight cars carrying nearly four hundred railroad employees, along with members of the Masonic Order. Engine 59, which

Effingham County During the Latter Nineteenth Century

carried the mourners, was draped in the "habiliments of woe." At Marshall, Casey and Greenup, others were added so that about five hundred people were on the train when it reached Effingham.

From a little white cottage about a half block from the Presbyterian church, Eames's coffin was carried to the church where the funeral sermon took place. About eleven o'clock, the Masons, both from Terre Haute and Effingham, gathered along with employees of the road and the members of the Brotherhood of Locomotive Engineers. Two long lines, which reached from the house to the church, provided a path through which the coffin was carried. Many family friends and community residents seemed to sympathize deeply with the sufferings of the young wife, whose painful mourning could be heard at a distance.

After the church service, the hearse and mourners' carriages—transporting members of the Masonic order in regalia, representatives of the Brotherhood of Locomotive Engineers, many employees of the line and numerous carriages—and a large group of citizens on foot made the journey to the cemetery, a mile and a half away. Although there was a slight drizzle, the immense crowd stood bareheaded by the grave while the ceremonies were in progress. The Reverend Mr. Pollock prayed; the Masonic ritual was read; an ode was sung; and then the coffin was lowered. After the minister pronounced the benediction, the crowd stood quite still for a second "as the clods began dropping upon the lid of the coffin, and the only sound mingling with their hollow knell, was the sobbing of the bereaved young wife. Then all dispersed and left the murdered man, the brave Engineer, to sleep out his sleep among the bleak hills of Illinois."

The crime that had led to the sad day was one of great notoriety in the annals of nineteenth-century crime. In fact, even by the 1890s, the murder of Milo Eames was still listed as among the twenty most important train robberies in the United States in the decades leading up to 1900.

At about 1:00 a.m. on July 9, 1875, the Vandalia route express train No. 5 pulled up to the Long Point, Illinois watering station, having passed through Effingham County only a matter of minutes before. After helping their cohorts uncouple the Adams express car on which payroll money was contained, two members of the robber band boarded the engine, pointed revolvers at Milo Eames and then demanded that he move the engine on down the tracks in an eastward direction. Eames seemed stupefied by the situation and did not respond to the orders. After making the demand to proceed and once again finding that the engineer would not obey, the outlaws did not hesitate in firing their weapons at him. One bullet passed through the heart, killing the engineer instantaneously. The other bullet struck a watch in the vest pocket of Eames. A newspaper account from the time period indicated that the train's fireman jumped to safety from the rear of the tender shortly before the robbers opened the throttle, full steam ahead. They did not realize that the airbrakes were set, causing the engine to stop about two miles down the track. At that point, when the train had come to a standstill, the robbers got off the engine and approached the express car, yelling to the messenger inside, a man named James Burk, to open the doors or be killed. He was prepared for them. He had barricaded the doors by throwing a heavy safe and large packages of freight against them, making it nearly impossible for the bandits to enter. He also had a revolver and was prepared for an attack. Burk yelled back that he would kill anyone who tried to enter the car.

A reporter wrote:

> At this the robbers began firing into the car. Finding this did not produce the desired effect, they commenced an assault upon the door with a crowbar, an axe and a sledge-hammer. For ten minutes they worked and pounded away like demons without producing any perceptible effect on the strong oak door. All at once the noise ceased and soon a party of passengers came up from the train which had been left behind, the robbers fleeing to the woods at their approach. Burke, still wishing to be on the safe side, refused to open the door. The party of passengers, among whom was Jack Vancleve an engineer in the employ of the road, got on board the engine, which was backed up and coupled to the train, but not until the train had reached Casey, the next station, would Burke open his doors. The body of the murdered engineer was found on the engine.

The authorities of the town of Casey, Illinois, offered $150 reward for the capture of the murderers, while the Vandalia Railroad Company offered $1,000 for their capture. Five men were arrested. A trial was held, but no one was ever convicted for the murder of Milo Eames.

A second major railroad-related event in Effingham County history during the latter nineteenth century also focused on the way in which railroad life was reflecting a "Wild West" spirit. Again, the event involved a nighttime robbery on the Vandalia line just slightly more miles away from Effingham, but in a westward direction. On October 29, 1874, Joseph Robbins, a watchman employed by the Vandalia Railway Company at the Kaskaskia bridge in Illinois, was murdered. The evidence all pointed toward Nathan

Effingham County During the Latter Nineteenth Century

Burgess, resident of the community of Vandalia. In court, newspapers recounted that he confessed due to the overwhelming evidence against him. He stated:

> *I knew the Vandalia pay-car had passed that afternoon and had paid Robbins his month's wages. I got that shot-gun and went to the bridge. As I approached the watch-house I saw through the window Robbins sitting inside; his shoulders and head only could be seen. I raised the gun and fired. I hesitated a few minutes to see if the report of the gun had aroused any one. I then went up to the watchhouse door, and found Robbins on his knees praying. I plainly heard him say: "Oh, God, have mercy on the one who did this! Spare him for Jesus' sake." I was horrified, and turned and ran, I didn't know where. I did not enter the house nor touch the door. His words haunt me still.*

Part of the tragedy was that Robbins was murdered for only $31.50. When the people of the area heard about the crime, there was great excitement in Fayette County. Because talk of lynching Burgess was everywhere, his

The only public execution in Effingham County history, the 1875 hanging of Nathan Burgess. *From* Fiftieth Anniversary Souvenir of Effingham, Illinois, *1903*.

lawyers asked for a change of venue. After moving the trial to Effingham, prosecutors proved that Burgess had committed the crime apparently for two reasons: one was to avenge an imaginary wrong and the other was to get money that he believed Robbins possessed. Upon conviction, Burgess was sentenced to die by hanging on the June 18, 1875. Again, there were many appeals to the governor asking for a pardon or a commutation of sentence, but nothing worked. Burgess was going to die.

As the time of the execution drew near, the city of Effingham took on a carnival-like atmosphere. A sense of excitement continued right up to the day of the trial as over two thousand people crowded into town. An old photograph taken on the day of the execution shows a large crowd, many of whom were children.

For the condemned man, the situation was quite somber, of course. One reporter for a Chicago paper described the convicted murderer's last hours on earth by writing:

> *Burgess, the doomed man, slept soundly from three- to six o'clock this morning when he arose, and at seven partook of a breakfast. He persisted all day in denying his guilt, although he heretofore published a confession he denied that he had written or caused the same to be written, and denounced it as a forgery. He was visited during the day by a minister of the gospel and other friends. He refused to join any sect. The execution took place in an enclosure, adjoining the Effingham Co. jail, shortly after two p.m., and was witnessed by probably fifty persons. He was led from his cell at 1:43 p.m. He walked up firmly, although not in a spirit of bravado and took a seat on the platform. A short prayer, the reading of death warrant, an interval of ten minutes for leave taking, adjustment of the noose, and Nathan Burgess was launched into eternity. His neck broke and pulsation ceased in 12 minutes. He died, protesting his innocence to the last and without pretense of religion.*

After the death of the prisoner, the huge throng was permitted to pass by the deceased's body.

Another chapter in Effingham County's history had been completed, as had an event that seemed like it belonged in the Wild West, not in a region of the country that was determined to become part of the economic boom of the Industrial Age.

The newspapers that had done such a good job reporting the criminal activity on the railroads had been part of the local culture since 1855, when the *Pioneer* was established in Ewington by W.B. Cooper. A new owner,

Effingham County During the Latter Nineteenth Century

Building inscription indicating the home of a nineteenth-century Effingham newspaper, the *Register*.

Colonel J.W. Filler, moved it to Effingham when that town became the county seat. During the Civil War, another new owner united the publication with another, the *Gazette*, which continued publication during the great national conflict. Then through a series of owners and name changes, the *Effingham Democrat* evolved and lasted for decades. Another newspaper published in Effingham was the *Register*, established in November 1864 as a Republican organ by Major William Haddock. It continued until 1872, when the paper, "having deflected to the support of Horace Greeley for President, on account of the loss of patronage, was compelled to suspend." A successor paper, the *Republican*, began publication during the fall of 1873. Although also experiencing a series of owners, this newspaper became a well-established part of the county seat community, offering an effective counter to the *Effingham Democrat* for many, many years.

In addition to the above, which were all English language newspapers, there was a paper printed for those who spoke German. The *Effingham Volksblatt* was established in the county seat during June 1878. The publication resulted from a visit to the area by General Herman Lieb of Chicago. Seeing the large number of German inhabitants in the countryside, the Chicagoan worked with Albert Gravenhorst of Effingham to provide local content for the seven-column paper. At first published in the Windy City and then in Milwaukee, by 1882, the paper was strictly printed locally. In 1883, Mr. Gravenhorst took ownership of the press and the building where it was issued. Politically, the paper advocated Democratic views. The German population of Effingham and adjoining counties helped Gravenhorst to be quite successful in his business venture.

Other communities in the county developed effective print media, as well. During the month of April 1863, a paper called the *Loyalist* (mentioned in Part Three) was established at Mason, Effingham County, by Mr. George Brewster. Because of its strong antislavery sentiment, the *Loyalist* stirred up a lot of hostility among the antiwar Democrats so that, after about seven months, the publisher suspended publication in Effingham and moved farther south, to Salem.

Altamont experienced a varied print media history during the latter nineteenth century. In May 1873, the *Altamont Courier* was established in the village by G.W. Grove, of Kimnundy, but was published only one year. In 1876, Loofbarrow & Humble established the *Altamont Telegram*. After being purchased by C.M. King the next year, the publication lasted until 1881. In December of the same year, C.F. Coleman and George M. LeCrone established the *Altamont News*, a very successful and lasting newspaper.

By the end of the century, several other newspapers were being read in other communities in the county. In 1898, the *Teutopolis Press* was established in Teutopolis by C.A. Worman and Henry Tegenkamp, with its first issue appearing April 21. Within a matter of days, Mr. Worman became the sole owner. This newspaper, like Gravenhorst's, became quite popular among citizens with German ancestry, as it sympathized politically with the Democrats. The *Special-Gazette*, of Dieterich, resulted from the combination of two publications: the *Special* and the *Gazette*, which for a time existed independently of each other. William Marra, J.N. Stroud, Arlen B. Wright and Frank Field were the names most associated with newspapers in the early years. The *Mason News* was established in 1896 under the ownership, management and editorship of two ladies, Misses Nettie Richmond and Susie Smith. This publication met with great success, being read in the small town where it was printed and in the surrounding countryside.

The 1910 *History of Effingham County, Illinois*, mentioned several other newspapers that were short-lived: the *Herald*, at Edgewood; the *Montrose Comet*, at Montrose; and an unnamed paper "published at Shumway for a short time."

Through those newspapers, the people learned how events in faraway places impacted on the local culture. In the pivotal year of 1875, reporters wrote:

> A number of German ecclesiastics and others, who had been driven out of the German empire by the operation of the Falk law, have arrived here [in New York City], and started for Teutopolis, Ill., via the Erie railroad, where they expect to find an asylum in the Catholic religious institution in

Effingham County During the Latter Nineteenth Century

that city. Among them are twelve priests and sixty ecclesiastical students, and fifteen families of different religious orders.

Bismarck's *Kulturkampf* was having impact on German Catholics, even those living thousands of miles away, on the Illinois prairie.

The same newspapers made the citizenry aware of the importance that state and national politicians attached to Effingham County. Two examples from the 1890s illustrated the point. First was John Peter Altgeld's attention given to Effingham County voters, both in 1892 and then again in 1896.

The year 1892 was the first time in Illinois's history that a foreign-born American citizen was a candidate for the highest office in the state. Most important for county residents was that Altgeld was far more than simply foreign-born: he was from Germany. In securing enough votes to be elected, John Peter Altgeld reached out to the various counties and communities that were of the same ethnic background as his own. Like many other political leaders, the Chicagoan, a person who would gain a place in American history books when he pardoned the Haymarket Square rioters, began to recognize that the sizeable German population found in the state represented a powerful voting bloc for any person who could appeal to the concerns of those who were of Teutonic origin.

Governor Altgeld, who spoke at Altamont and Effingham to appeal to the German voters in 1896. *From* Portrait and Biographical Record of Effingham, Jasper and Richland Counties, *1893*.

One newspaper account described the way in which the local visits were carried out:

> *When he enters a city he does not confine himself to interviews with the leaders and prominent members of the party, but without any bluster or fuss goes among the shops and chats to the workingmen like a plain, every-day sort of a man. He never fails to call upon every German minister, and quickly enlists his favor through the school law question, which is proving such a Republican boomerang. A German is always drawn to another German, and the memory of the "vaterland" is a tie that never breaks. Judge Altgeld interests himself in the affairs of each German church and parish and when he leaves has a warm supporter in the minister, and through his influence substantially a solid endorsement of the Germans in that town.*

His 1892 visit to Altamont demonstrated that winning strategy.

In the days leading up to Altgeld's visit, the people for miles around Altamont began planning for the political rally. In Moccasin, Blue Point, Beecher City, Effingham and Teutopolis, special delegations assembled to attend the speech, which Democrats hoped would bind together all people of Germanic origin.

The crowd that jammed into Altamont was huge. With sidewalks and stores overflowing with people (local newspaper accounts indicated that somewhere between six and ten thousand people had come to listen to the man who would become governor of the Prairie State), when Altgeld spoke the audience was wildly enthusiastic. It was clear that Effingham County's German population was going to vote for the man who shared their cultural interests.

John Peter Altgeld went on to defeat the incumbent governor, Joseph Fifer, 425,558 to 402,676 votes. To historians, a major factor in Altgeld's victory was the defection of many Germans who had voted for Republicans in earlier elections.

As governor, Altgeld gained national notoriety, which served to create a negative public opinion against the former Prussian. Even those who supported his reform-minded measures—such as a women's eight-hour law, an act prohibiting discrimination against union members and a factory inspection law—often had serious reservations about the wisdom demonstrated by the governor both in the Haymarket Square pardon and in the Pullman strike.

The 1896 political season served to test whether Altgeld still had the ability to create another winning strategy. The same election also brought Governor

Effingham County During the Latter Nineteenth Century

John P. Altgeld back to Effingham County—this time to the courthouse steps in mid-October.

A special train carrying the governor's party traveled on a hurried schedule across southern Illinois as he visited Robinson, Lawrenceville, Mount Carmel, Eldorado, Vienna, Mound City and Cairo. On the morning of October 13, the "special" had allowed the governor to talk to voters in East St. Louis, Collinsville, Greenville and St. Elmo, as the politically astute German steamed toward the county where so many people had shown great enthusiasm almost exactly four years earlier. He saw nothing to indicate that his popularity in Effingham County had waned at all.

From the time he arrived at the depot at 1:00 p.m., where fifteen hundred people awaited him, through the time of thunderous cheering as he was escorted along Banker and Jefferson Streets to the courthouse square, until he finally stood on the steps of the center of county government, Altgeld was the recipient of massive affection from the citizenry of this county. Some estimated that upward of ten thousand people had assembled to hear the governor. His half-hour-long speech brought many cheers from the crowd. A local correspondent described the speech as "masterful" and as one that "showed that the speaker felt every word he uttered."

But the larger question was whether that veneration was representative of the whole state of Illinois. In a matter of a few weeks, the November election revealed the answer. It was a stunning defeat for Altgeld and his fellow Democrats.

A second major politician who visited Effingham, this one a presidential candidate, was William Jennings Bryan. In the aftermath of his 1896 nomination as the candidate of the Democratic Party, the "Great

Four-time presidential candidate William Jennings Bryan, frequent speaker at the courthouse. *From* Great Issues and National Leaders, *1908.*

Commoner" traveled through his birthplace state. The newspapers recorded that "the crowd at Effingham was small but it was enthusiastic." Bryan consented to make a speech. Not leaving the train, but standing on the rear platform, he spoke of visiting the community less than a year earlier to speak at the courthouse. He then focused on the successes of having his views become part of the party's official stances, views on matters such as "free silver," a popular notion in Effingham County. Within minutes, even though Bryan was not finished with his thoughts, the train moved out amidst great cheering for the candidate and his wife.

The next stop was Edgewood. Once again, a group of local residents crowded around the station, trying to be part of the fairly substantial number who shook hands with the famous orator. A display of fireworks made the whistle-stop rather memorable for all involved.

During the next several years, well into the twentieth century, Mr. Bryan returned to Effingham County on multiple occasions to meet his supporters.

Part of the reason for politicians visiting the area was the fact that it seemed to show great prospects for economic growth. There were numerous sturdy buildings being constructed in all parts of the county during the late nineteenth century. New locations for businesses, entertainment, education, worship and private residences dotted the countryside.

Altamont building built in the latter nineteenth century.

Effingham County During the Latter Nineteenth Century

Right: The Crews National Bank, Montrose.

Below: Cornerstone of the Altamont Methodist Church.

Dr. Wright mansion at Altamont, listed on the National Register of Historical Sites.

The best example of the last-mentioned type of construction can still be seen in Altamont—the residence of Dr. Charles M. Wright I. He provided the county with one of two buildings that are today listed on the National Register of Historic Places. He demonstrated the economic success that many in the county experienced during the late 1800s.

As mentioned in the earlier story about Joseph Boleyjack, Dr. Wright knew the Ewington and Freemanton region quite well as a "saddlebag doctor," but he realized that those communities were in a state of decline after the completion of the Terre Haute, Vandalia and St. Louis Railroad. He also saw that when Altamont was settled at the intersection of the Vandalia Line with the Ohio and Mississippi Railroad, there would be need for his services in that location.

By 1870, when he was only thirty-six years old, Dr. Wright had a total worth of slightly over $20,000, a considerable sum for that era on the frontier. With his finances, he purchased lots in Altamont. He built a large two-story structure in which he located his medical office and, later on, a bank on the first floor. On the second level of the building, he provided a large hall with a stage, commonly known as the Wright Opera House, a place where "civic, school and other gatherings" occurred. He also built a

Effingham County During the Latter Nineteenth Century

residence in 1871, in which his family lived until 1889, when the spacious Wright mansion was constructed. The home, late Victorian in style, with eighteen rooms—including seven bedrooms, a full basement and a large attic with high ceilings—was a beautiful addition to the town.

The house was built to be self-sufficient, so there was an artificial gaslight system, indoor plumbing with water provided by a double cistern, a central steam system and windows with the year of construction etched into them. The total cost for materials and labor was approximately $35,000.

The luxurious house was clear evidence that Effingham County had prosperous people by the end of the nineteenth century. It also had individuals who caused national and international attention to be focused on the region because of the genius that they demonstrated.

Some of the county's residents were destined for fame during the late nineteenth century and beyond. The Kepley and Ellis families were among that number. The first became well known as temperance advocates and

Downtown Effingham monument recognizes Ada and Henry Kepley.

Altamont's Union Cemetery stone for the community's only African American family.

women's rights advocates. The second family had a member, for many years a barber in Altamont, whose diaries of the life of African Americans in an all-white midwestern town gained recognition during the latter twentieth century. The life stories of these families could fill volumes.

Two other prominent citizens during the 1890s and beyond were nationally known during their lifetimes. Both were children during the Civil War. One was the son of a physician living in Mason; the other was the son of a Presbyterian minister from Effingham.

The son of the physician became a medical doctor but gained national recognition as a skilled literary figure praised by some of the most famous authors and poets in the late 1800s. The minister's son became a photographer who established a school of photography that attracted students from around the globe. Both of their stories are interesting.

James Newton Matthews was born in Putnam County, near Greencastle, Indiana, on May 27, 1852. He was only two years old when his father moved the family to Mason, Illinois. From childhood on, it was clear to those who knew the youngster that he had a special gift. He liked to read and write, especially words that rhymed. Many thought the literary interest came from his father, who penned articles for local newspapers, medical literature and the like. During the Civil War, young James worked in the office of the *Loyalist*, Mason's strongly Unionist newspaper. It was the perfect place to enhance his skills and interest.

James Newton Matthews has a special place in the history of the University of Illinois, for he was the very first student to enroll at that prestigious academic location. After graduating as number one in his class in 1872, the young man wrote for a variety of publications, demonstrating his writing skill for a period of three years. But, in the aftermath of the death of his father, the young man, in 1875, entered the Medical College of St. Louis and graduated, again, first in his class. In 1878, after marrying Miss Luella Brown of Madison, Indiana, the couple located in Mason to begin the practice of medicine. To the townspeople, he became much beloved as a small-town doctor who was devoted to his patients.

Popular local physician and nationally acclaimed poet James Newton Matthews, resident at Mason. *From* Effingham County School History, *1918*.

But there was another part of his life that played out on a much larger screen. James Newton Matthews was deeply involved in the literary life of America, especially that of the Midwest. Although others had mentioned the creation of an association of writers from the middle part of the United States, it was the Mason doctor whose proposal led to the creation of a group known as the "Western Association of Writers." Initially, he thought only poetic writers from Illinois and Indiana should be part of the assemblage, but later he broadened his ideas to include writers from Ohio, Michigan, Wisconsin and other states.

The first convention of the group was held in Indianapolis in 1886, with Matthews serving as vice-president. Within the context of the association,

Matthews formed a lifelong friendship with the great Hoosier poet James Whitcomb Riley, a person who, along with James Newton, served to encourage the first major African American poet, Paul Dunbar, to develop his literary gift. Each summer for many years after its establishment, the Western Association of Writers brought together the best literary minds of the Midwest.

Matthews contributed poetry to numerous national and local newspapers, as well as to some leading magazines and journals. His topics were as varied as his interests in life—nature, history, biography, rural life and medicine.

In 1888, with the publication of his first book, a collection of his poems, his hometown became the center of a celebration in which the accolades for the beloved doctor and poet were more numerous than anyone could have imagined. *Tempe Vale* was a fascinating collection of the writer who was nicknamed "The Poet of the Prairies."

James Newton Matthews continued to be active to the end of his days, writing poems focused on local concerns—for example, the building of Effingham's Central School—or about local people whose lives inspired him and about nearly every topic that is part of the human experience. He even wrote lyrics for sheet music and contributed to *Readings and Recitations for Primary School*, a popularly used book in public school systems. He served as a popular speaker across Indiana and Illinois, as well.

When he died in March 1910, the *Mason News* presented his obituary, which began:

> *After an attendance of almost constant attendance on the sick and exposure from going from place to place at all hours of the day and night, Dr. J.N. Matthews took down sick with a complication of pneumonia and heart trouble, Tuesday, March 1st, and, as the week wore on and people realized that he was fighting a losing battle with the grim reaper Death, the anxiety seemed written on every face. And when on the next Monday, March 7th, word was passed from one to another that he was gone, hearts seemed to stand still and the community was grief stricken, many feeling that they had lost a friend, a brother, a relative.*

Effingham County had lost one of its treasures.

Another outstanding example of the county's citizens was Lewis Bissell, a gentleman who moved to Effingham County in 1864 when his father, Reverend Sanford Bissell, and his mother, Sarah Bissell, moved to the county seat to establish a Presbyterian congregation. Although his parents' influence

Effingham County During the Latter Nineteenth Century

"Poet of the Prairies" gravestone, Union Cemetery, Mason.

was great in the locality, the son, in his adult years, influenced photography around the world. By 1902, one national photographic magazine stated: "The Illinois College of Photography, at Effingham, Illinois is without doubt one of the best, if not the best, equipped photographic colleges in this country." Numbers of photographic magazines indicated that the school was surpassed in quality of study only by two other photographic colleges in New York City.

Lewis H. Bissell, born on June 29, 1859, was educated both in the public schools and in the private school conducted by his father in Effingham County's seat of government. From an early age, by age fourteen to be precise, the youngster had demonstrated his genius as a photographer. By adulthood, one author wrote about him: "To the development of the art-science of Photography Mr. Bissell is what Mergenthaler is to the type-machine, and Edison to electricity."

By age sixteen, young Bissell had demonstrated an unusual business talent that worked hand in hand with his photographic skill. The result was that for one year he was both a financial and working partner with William Lawson, a local photographer. The next year, the photographic prodigy joined forces with Thomas Lyon; in his eighteenth year, he briefly was an independent businessman in the photographer's trade. His nineteenth year witnessed a Mr. Rankin becoming a business partner with Bissell in a longer-lasting business relationship. When Bissell finally launched a career on his own, although in a nineteen-year period of time eighteen other photographers tried unsuccessfully to offer competition for him, not one of them competed successfully with the gallery, which was recognized as "the largest and best equipped" between "Chicago and New Orleans." The simple fact was that Lewis H. Bissell delivered high-quality photographic work.

By the beginning the last decade of the century, Bissell wanted ever greater challenges. As a strong supporter of higher education, the talented photographer actively joined with other prominent citizens in the creation of Effingham's Austin College, an institution for which he served as a trustee.

But Austin College was a liberal arts school catering to a wide variety of educational studies. Because Bissell wanted to provide an unsurpassed educational experience for people who shared his devotion to all phases of the photography trade, in 1893, the Effingham photographer began to make his dream a reality. The Illinois College of Photography was born. He wanted to provide "a school of practical training under the direction of photographers of national reputation," as well as to afford students "unequaled facilities" where they were able to receive thorough training to prepare them for their life's work. With that mission in mind, Bissell developed an educational facility consisting of both a college of photo engraving and a college of photography, collectively known as the Illinois College of Photography.

The 1902 Annual Report of the Commissioner of Labor contained a glowing statement regarding the success of the Illinois College of Photography. The commissioner noted that the school had grown from 1 student in 1893 to an annual enrollment of more than 250 in the early twentieth century; furthermore, the commissioner noted that the graduates commanded high wages. Other specialists in the field of education verified the validity of the praise. Lewis Flader, president of the International Union of Photo-engravers, visited the college in 1903 to view the equipment in the engraving department. He was well satisfied with what he saw. By 1920, Catherine Filene, editor of the book *Careers for Women*, included the statement: "From the standpoint of the artistic photographer the best school for portrait work is Clarence H. White's in New York. There are two others in New York which give more of a commercial training, and one in Effingham Illinois...Illinois College of Photography, 910 Wabash Avenue, Effingham, Illinois."

Bissell's schools had achieved high degrees of success in several important qualities that they, through the influence of their founder, had. First, the faculty, though relatively small, was made up of creative people who knew the subject of photography quite well. Professors D.J. Cook and Felix Raymer were men of national repute due to their journal articles. The college magazine, *The Bissellonian*, described Cook as a regular contributor to *Photo Era*, "considered one of the world's leading photographic magazines." Professor Raymer was a popular speaker at photography conventions, as well as the author of articles that his co-photographers found to be immensely practical. The *St. Louis and Canadian Photographer* magazine declared that his name was "a household word among the fraternity" of photo artists.

The Illinois College of Photography's success also grew from the use of the latest technology. A few months after Roentgen had demonstrated X-ray photography, President Bissell demonstrated his knowledge of the subject by locating a sewing needle that an Effingham woman had embedded in her hand. In similar fashion, shortly after McDonough discovered the process for producing color photos, in 1898 the Illinois College of Photography had a process of its own and was able to "reproduce all the colors of the rainbow with the camera."

The college's great success also resulted from the founder's extensive use of advertising throughout the nation and world. Many foreign students came to the little Illinois town to learn the photography trade. Although a high percentage of the ads were in photographic magazines, Bissell also advertised in popular journals, such as the mass-market *Munsey's Magazine*. The potential student read descriptions of the beautiful campus with its state-of-the-art facilities, as well as the testimonies of former students who praised the quality of the education that they had received. From their testimonies, it was evident that the ICP grads were loyal to their alma mater.

Although Lewis Bissell disappeared from the leadership of the Illinois College of Photography, the school stayed in existence until 1931, when because of economic hardships typical of the era of the Great Depression, the educational enterprise, on August 8, closed its doors. Lewis H. Bissell's grand achievement had come to an end, but his influence continued in the former students whose photography galleries were scattered around the world.

Effingham County was a vastly different place from what it had been when the Bissell family had moved there more than a generation earlier.

PART 5

EFFINGHAM COUNTY, EARLY 1900S UNTIL MID-CENTURY

The events of the first half of the twentieth century brought times of unity and excitement as well as times of tension and tragedy. Whatever the circumstance, the period reflected the nineteenth-century history of the county. Sometimes the events reflected the ethnic heritage; other times the events reflected the strength of character of the early pioneers.

Effingham County, of course, had a large percentage of the population whose ancestry was German. Traveling across the county today, one sees reminders of that Germanic heritage, whether in terms of the German phrases carved onto gravestones or in words found on cornerstones of various churches. Many churches in Effingham County used German as the fundamental language for services. There were, of course, the German Catholic churches and German Lutheran churches, as well as German Methodist churches. That deeply instilled German heritage was passed to generations following the initial immigrant groups.

Early in the twentieth century, area German Roman Catholics were thrilled when the county seat was chosen as the location for the fifteenth annual meeting of the Federation of German Catholic Societies of Illinois. In mid-May 1907, over 1,500 conventioneers, with their spouses, flocked to Effingham to the convention hosted by St. Anthony German Catholic Church. The city had hung a large banner high above Effingham's Jefferson Avenue boldly proclaiming "Willkommen Delegaten." The Germanic culture dominated the next several days.

Effingham County, Early 1900s Until Mid-Century

Above: German language inscription, St. Paul's Lutheran Church, rural Montrose.

Right: German language gravestone in Edgewood Cemetery.

St. Paul's Lutheran Church, Altamont.

Cornerstone of St. John's Lutheran Church near Dieterich.

Effingham County, Early 1900s Until Mid-Century

Some members of the Bethlehem Lutheran Church migrated during the Great German Migration.

Typically, the federation had only selected larger cities as the location for the gathering, so the decision to locate in a relatively small community was quite an honor, as evidenced by Effingham mayor John Shea's appeal to the citizens of the community during the week immediately preceding the event. In a local newspaper, he wrote: "In order to evidence our appreciation of the visitors, I hereby urgently request that on this occasion all business houses in the city, as well as residences, especially, those along the line of parade, be decorated with our national colors, and the streets cleared of all rubbish, thereby paying our respects to our guests." The city responded on an incredible scale.

Excitement was in the air, not only in Effingham County but throughout the state of Illinois as well. When the Wabash Railroad organized a special excursion train to bring visitors to Effingham from the Springfield and Decatur areas, hundreds of tickets were quickly sold.

When the delegations arrived in the host city, they found a simply beautiful day and a city filled with people anxious to attend the opening day's session of the fifteenth annual convention of the German Societies of Illinois. The town looked great.

Prior to an excursion train from Decatur, the largest delegation that had arrived was from Sigel. Over two hundred in number, they had come to town on the eight o'clock passenger train, bubbling with enthusiasm. By noon, Effingham was filled with people lining the streets. When the conventioneers saw the huge German-language banner welcoming them, there was no question that the community was glad to have five or six thousand visitors.

The convention formalities were begun when President William Rauen of Chicago called the meeting to order, and then Effingham resident B.R.

St. Anthony German Catholic Church, Effingham, host of the 1907 German Catholic convention. *From* Souvenier und Programm Der 15. General-Versammlung Des Deutschen Katholischen Vereins-Bundes von Illinois.

Wolters, as president of the local committees, and Reverend Lammert, pastor of the St. Anthony congregation, welcomed the guests, in short German addresses. Following those greetings, John Shea, mayor of the city, spoke:

> *I can assure you, my friends, that every citizen of Effingham feels highly honored by your coming here, representing, as you do, the German Catholic population of all walks of life in the great state of Illinois.*
>
> *...As you have perhaps heard and doubtless personally observed, Effingham is but a small place; however, we have several enterprising men in our midst who take great interest in her advancement, and feel a natural pride in having our good old town do its best on occasions of this kind.*
>
> *To be brief, as chief executive of our little city, I cheerfully hand you over its keys and every man, woman and child in Effingham knows, they could not be given into better hands. I sincerely hope that God will crown your deliberations with unqualified success.*

Effingham County, Early 1900s Until Mid-Century

After each delegate had received an official badge and souvenir, along with a ticket to the Sunday evening performance by St. Anthony's Dramatic Club, the officers and delegates formed a line and marched over to the parish house, where they met the Right Reverend John Jansen, bishop of Belleville. Following the bishop's celebration of a pontifical high mass, Father Pennartz of nearby Sigel delivered the German sermon for the occasion.

Following mealtime, by 2:00 p.m., 1,000 members of the society from throughout the state formed a line nearly a mile long so that by 2:30, they were ready to begin walking the parade route, a distance of nearly three miles. With at least 1,500 in the parade itself, the event was one of "the finest spectacles ever seen in this city," as one reporter wrote. The lengthy formation of the parade was led by the local police, and then followed by the marshal of the day, B. Overbeck, and staff, and then the flag-bearers with the American flag, followed by groups representing at least seventeen parishes, both from the area and throughout the state. There were numerous church officials, along with priests and, finally, citizens on horseback and in carriages. Sometimes the parade line led through the country with the marchers having oat fields and cornfields on both sides of their route.

One newspaper story indicated: "At one place the Goodman band stopped out behind a barn on the edge of an oat field and played a selection which reverberated through the surrounding country and brought people from several miles around to hear and see them."

After the parade was concluded, the afternoon services began. There were at least three messages delivered to the group; the choir presented several selections, along with two solos by Father Hoffman, a priest with quite a reputation for his vocal ability. The local parishioners were proud when they heard the visitors rave about "the finely decorated interior of St. Anthony church; the well arranged building and especially, what won over the hearts of the young, a well-appointed stage." Father Hoffman was the recipient of special praise for his efforts in that regard, as was Henry Stockman and his committee, who had been responsible for decorating all parish buildings.

The convention continued into the evening hours on Sunday with open meetings at St. Anthony's Hall. There was also an English lecture that the public could attend, as well as a concert at 7:00 p.m. by the Goodman Band on the school grounds.

Beginning on Monday morning, the openness of the meetings changed somewhat. After a high mass and a message to the delegates, typical convention business was carried out during the rest of the day.

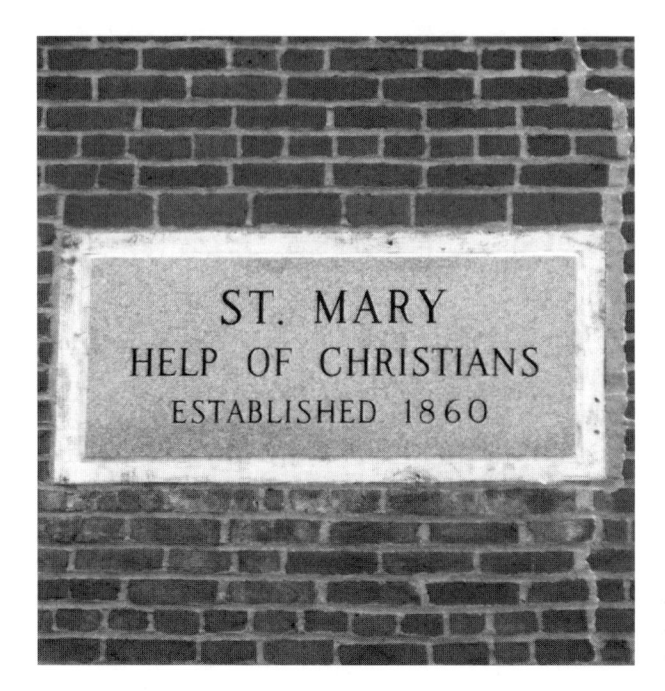

St. Mary Help of Christians Roman Catholic Church, Green Creek.

Monday night witnessed the presentation of the drama *Capital vs. Labor* by the St. Anthony's Dramatic Club. The local opera house orchestra showed off its talent by accompanying the actors with music, which added drama to the lines.

Tuesday morning opened with solemn memorial services for the repose of the souls of the departed members of the federation and then continued the business session. Although that Tuesday afternoon was a rainy one, the delegates were provided a most memorable time. Immediately after dinner, about thirty German farmers brought their surreys to the sheds east of the church, where they waited for officers and delegates who wanted to travel to Teutopolis. By four o'clock in the afternoon, some one hundred of the delegates and officers were in the little German village.

The delegates were delighted upon their arrival, as they were surrounded on all sides by the national and church colors and a special greeting: "Ehre dem den Ehre gebuehrt." With the church bells ringing, at the entrance to the hall they were cordially met by "the good old Father Casimir himself, whose sincere welcome was a treat in itself."

Once in the hall, the elderly priest gave them an enthusiastic welcome, followed by a German play (*Peter's Finish*) presented by the dramatic club; immediately thereafter there was a drill by the girls. The crowd repeatedly

Effingham County, Early 1900s Until Mid-Century

and loudly cheered the efforts of both boys and girls because it was such an enjoyable time. After this special time, the company went into the hall below and was given what was called a royal "Dutch Lunch."

Several of the delegates remained in Teutopolis until late in the afternoon, visiting the church and the college in which the town took so much pride.

The Effingham *Democrat* reported, "After supper, Father Hoffman and the *Bewirthungs Comite* treated the guests to pleasant hours in the Tyrolese Alps at St. Anthony's Hall, wherein a smoker given. The Opera House Orchestra furnished some excellent music, and the Tiroler Quartette rendered some choice German songs."

Many delegates stayed until quite late in the night; in fact, some of them remained until Wednesday morning. By Wednesday afternoon, it was time to bring the fifteenth annual convention of the German Societies of Illinois to a close. Some of the delegates who had attended many of the meetings of the societies in previous years had nothing but praise for what they had experienced in Effingham County. It was a grand celebration of the local Germanic heritage.

There were other times of excitement in the county during the early part of the twentieth century. One of grandest was when the Liberty Bell came to Effingham County. The occasion that brought the historic artifact to the area was the Panama-Pacific International Exposition, the 1915 World's Fair, held in San Francisco, California. It was on the bell's ten-day journey back to the East Coast that it came through Effingham County.

It made numerous stops. Everywhere the welcome was the same—great excitement, great patriotic feelings filled the air. In St. Louis, 100,000 gathered to see the icon. On November 21, 1915, throngs gathered in Greenville and then in Vandalia to see the magnificent symbol. Then the train began eastward once again, this time into Effingham County. There were stops at Altamont, Effingham and Teutopolis, where a writer for the *Teutopolis Press* penned:

> *Many of our patriotic citizens together with the students of St. Joseph's College were at the station to view and salute the historic bell, and the joy and enthusiasm shown by the crowd was proof of the honor in which the relic is held by American citizens. Flags were waved and the loud shouts and hurrahs kindled again the flames of the love of the native land known to all as patriotism.*
>
> *The Bell was carried on an open flat car in full view of all and was decorated with flowers and the presence of the national emblem, fitfully blowing from all four corners of the car.*

Effingham County

This joyous event took place, of course, during the First World War (although the United States had not yet entered the conflict), an era when the United States witnessed great economic and social costs. Occasions laden with joy could readily be followed by those that were filled with deep grief. The unity of citizens often was destroyed by suspicion regarding loyalty to the war effort.

Although the war seemed far away from the United States in terms of geography, it soon became a focus of discussion throughout the countryside. The warring powers were nations that had contributed many immigrants to the population of our land.

As with most wars, public opinion was divided. There were those who argued in favor of assisting the Allies and those who believed in giving support to the Central Powers. That debate became quite localized as people suspected their neighbors and fellow citizens whose lineage was different from their own. Of course, regions and counties that had high concentrations of persons descended from German-speaking immigrants were a main focus of public discussion. Effingham County was very much a part of the national war effort both in terms of soldiers who fought and in terms of the valiant effort found on the homefront, as well as in terms of the suspicion of those of German descent.

After Congress passed the Selective Service Act authorizing the president to call men into military service, the Selective Service System began the process of selecting young males for induction into military service. Just like the situation during the Civil War, each state had to contribute a certain number of soldiers. State authorities in turn then determined allotments for the political subdivisions.

Local boards with the task of registering, providing serial and order numbers, classifying and finally calling the draftees into the national service were established in each county. Initially 1,356 registered in 1917 in Effingham County. By war's end, Effingham draft officials had issued 3,702 selective cards.

Soon, participation in the war effort became part of the news. A Racine, Wisconsin newspaper toward the end of May 1917 reported that "Dieterich, Effingham county, Ill., the center of a German-speaking community, has a population of 600 and has enrolled seventy-six in a machine-gun company being organized for the Fourth Illinois infantry." By the fall of the year, news stories focused on area soldiers being trained in Texas or awaiting orders for deployment into battle areas. With deployment, of course, also came the news of battle casualties.

A news headline screamed "Effingham Boy Dies in France" and then went on to talk about Sergeant Rutherford Alcock, son of Mrs. Ada Alcock

Effingham County, Early 1900s Until Mid-Century

Summit township World War I soldier.

of Effingham, a twenty-year-old who had enlisted in Effingham and was a member of Company C, 130th Infantry, at the time of his death. Another news story told that "relatives of Lewis Brewster of Montrose received word that he died...in France on the western battle front. He went with one of the drafted men's companies from Effingham." Still another article dealt with the activities of three local soldiers who also were brothers—Clem, Leo and John Wiedman, all members of the 130th Infantry. Two of the three were severely wounded.

Similar news items were repeated time and again in the local and statewide press. Many soldiers paid the supreme sacrifice.

There was also much activity on the local homefront. Patriotic rallies were held periodically to honor the war effort, such as one held by members of the Daughters of the American Revolution in October 1917 at the Effingham Methodist Church. The families of the men in Company G, which was then in Texas, were guests of honor. Another show of patriotism occurred on October 9, 1917, when nearly two thousand schoolchildren from the county's fifty schools marched in the Effingham County School Rally Day, a gathering of unquestionable success. As those children marched, a crowd estimated at nearly six thousand lined the parade route. The state superintendent of schools, Francis Blair, delivered a well-received speech. During the afternoon, contests were held to build a spirit of devotion and a sense of community.

The war required money, so a lot of energy went into fundraising efforts such as selling Liberty Loan Bonds. In the fall of 1917, Effingham County took much pride in the fact that the citizens were $3,000 over their goal. Local employees of the Pennsylvania Railroad had purchased over $5,000 worth of bonds by themselves. This fundraising success continued until the war's end. In July 1919, a headline boasted "EFFINGHAM LEADS IN W.S.S. SALES" and then went on to say that Effingham County was at the top on a list of sixty-three counties in the sale of war saving stamps during the month of May of that year. The total sold was $2,575.73. Other monetary support was not on as large a scale. For instance, in September 1917, a card party was held at the armory to raise money for the Company G fund.

The county was determined to show the soldiers that the local area supported them. When local National Guard units left for camp, local businesses closed down.

The Red Cross demonstrated similar community spirit through its membership drives. The county was very supportive of humanitarian work. At the end of September 1917, in one week the women of the Effingham chapter of the Red Cross collected $85.10, a considerable sum for the time. The money was used to purchase comfort kits for the soldiers. Local merchants cooperated with the Red Cross workers and allowed the women to have the articles for use in the kit bags at wholesale prices, or about $1.35 for each bag.

Besides the money-raising efforts, there were other types of homefront sacrifices: on July 26, 1918, the fuel administrator for Illinois notified the county fuel administrator that Effingham County, along with all the counties in the southern part of the state, could not be supplied with any anthracite or hard coal for the coming winter.

All these items were part of normal day-to-day activities for area residents. Other circumstances were not. But they were significant, for they showed the degree of patriotic spirit that existed in Effingham County during World War I.

Effingham County, Early 1900s Until Mid-Century

One rather unusual story concerned a major world figure who came to Effingham via the railroad. Marshal Joseph Joffre, the very popular French chief of staff who was considered the "Savior of France" after the First Battle of the Marne, was traveling in Illinois as part of a major effort to get American support for the Allied cause. After a big celebration at Decatur, the mission started on its way again, but when it got near Arcola, the train derailed. Although railway officials believed they could easily account for the accident, some of the French Commission members suspected that area German plotters had caused the crash. An Arcola farm boy added to that suspicion when he spoke about seeing a mysterious man near the wreck scene a short while before the accident.

Very quickly, another train was sent to the site to carry the delegation on its way toward Effingham County, where they arrived in the pre-dawn hours. Long before daylight, small groups of people began to gather about the Effingham station in the hope of obtaining a glimpse of the international guests. The French officials stayed long enough to permit local citizens to greet the distinguished visitors, and then they were on their way east into Indiana as their goodwill journey continued.

The suspicion that surrounded the train wreck was quite typical of much of the United States during the First World War. Persons of German ancestry were thought to be potential threats to this country. A strong spirit of intolerance was in the air. Everything German was suspect, whether that was the German language, German religious services or even German food.

Hatred of things German abounded, and that hatred was often close at hand. On a certain Sunday in October 1917, a funeral service at the Lutheran church in Shumway was marred by an altercation over the choice of undertakers. The undertaker, a member of a committee to stop potential German sympathizers from sabotaging the war effort, had severely criticized the pastor of the congregation, charging that the minister had uttered seditious statements on more than one occasion. The ill feeling between the two led to an embarrassing display of bad conduct on the day of the funeral.

Locally, the focus often was on churches. There was suspicion of German Lutheran churches, German Methodist churches and German Catholic churches. All these groups, of course, were well represented in Effingham County and in surrounding counties. Anything that could be interpreted as un-American was sure to bring a sharp exchange. By early May 1918, rumors were circulating about outbreaks of anti-American feelings by local pro-German residents. Although the allegations were denied by local authorities, it was difficult to stop them completely.

Later that same year, Effingham County residents were shocked to read a report in a Decatur newspaper stating: "Rumor has it that Professor Charles, the Englishman who attended the Bissell colleges and who afterwards taught music and drawing in this city for several years, has been imprisoned as a German spy."

The classic example of the intolerance, however, was found in the suspicion directed against Teutopolis, which was, according to W.H. Kerrick, a federal official who was assigned to Effingham County, "the hotbed of and stormcenter of all the anti-American and pro-German plotting and agitation" in Effingham County, a county that contained "the most dangerous pro-German group in the whole state of Illinois."

Theodosius Plassmeyer, pastor of the Teutopolis church during the World War I era, wrote a detailed account of the incident. According to the priest, soon after President Woodrow Wilson's reelection in 1916, propaganda generated by the federal Committee for Public Information stirred great hostility toward everything German. The hatred was further stirred by local feelings, such as that evidenced in an article published in a Newton, Illinois newspaper. Charges against Teutopolis were quite mean-spirited and caused deep resentment within the community.

A public letter-writing exchange ensued. Then two strangers appeared in the Effingham County town. The men indicated they were in the area as vacationers who wanted to do a little hunting and fishing, but their stay consisted of a number of visits to the various businesses in the village. They asked a lot of questions regarding how the local citizens felt about the war. Father Plassmeyer got involved by delivering an eloquent sermon dealing with Christian citizenship and the need for people to be patriotic. Shortly after Plassmeyer's message, the two men disappeared as quickly as they had arrived; but Mr. Kerrick came onto the scene.

On the very day the federal agent arrived in the town, Pastor Plassmeyer and the local teachers, the Notre Dame Sisters, had the schoolchildren participate in a large Decoration Day (today's Memorial Day) celebration. Patriotism was the central theme. There was a parade with American flags in fantastic numbers. There were uplifting, patriotic songs galore; then came the special ceremony at the cemetery, during which the schoolchildren decorated the graves of soldiers from the Civil War and Spanish-American War. Mr. Kerrick saw firsthand the loyalty and devotion that the townspeople had for the United States of America, their land in which they took great pride.

In the aftermath of the great celebration, Father Plassmeyer still had to answer the other charges that Kerrick had been ordered to investigate.

Effingham County, Early 1900s Until Mid-Century

All those charges were easily discounted by the priest as he discussed the character of the people of his parish. There was no need to fear that Teutopolis would be a center of enemy sabotage.

The citizens of Effingham County showed their colors—literally and figuratively, the county demonstrated that it was true red, white and blue. The county's population seemed united by its patriotism. That unity was especially needed ten years after the signing of the Versailles Treaty brought the First World War to an end in 1919.

The year 1929 brought the collapse of the stock market and, with it, economic collapse throughout the land. The reminders of the Great Depression are located across the county in a variety of ways, including bronze plates attached to the walls of schools or other public buildings and concrete reliefs on the sides of buildings indicating the date of construction. By themselves, those reminders of the past once again serve as mind-flints to spark an interest in the story of Effingham County residents who experienced the troubling times between the collapse of the stock market and the beginning of World War II.

Effingham County was almost one hundred years old when the Great Depression hit America. The fear that gripped the nation after the stock market crash of 1929 did not reach Effingham County immediately. Few residents owned stocks anyway, and the tight-fisted, predominantly German populace had steered clear of debt and installment buying and other reckless business practices of the 1920s.

The county's one daily newspaper, the *Daily Record*, did not mention the October crash; instead, typical news articles by 1930 discussed "Effingham's Growing Pains" and proclaimed the local economy sound and healthy. Since all previous depressions had bypassed Effingham County, leaders assumed there was nothing about which to be concerned.

One-third of the county's nineteen thousand people lived in either the county seat of Effingham or about twelve miles west in Altamont. The rest lived on small farms or in towns like Edgewood, Mason, Funkhouser, Beecher City, Shumway, Watson and Teutopolis, villages which, with the exception of Teutopolis, had entered a period of decline in the 1920s, when Governor Len Small had set several road-building records in Illinois. Shoppers traveled these new roads into Effingham, Altamont or Teutopolis for a better selection of merchandise. Community spirit remained high in the smaller towns nonetheless.

The industrial and manufacturing potential offered by the railroads and paved roads went untapped by Effingham County until after World War II.

Meanwhile, most income came from agriculture. Lack of a strong industrial base helped cushion the Depression's impact, since there were few businesses around to close their doors.

Major employers included Siemer's Flour Mill in Teutopolis, which bought wheat from a fifty-mile radius for milling top-quality flour; the J.M. Schultz Seed Company in Dieterich, which ranked among Illinois's largest wholesale seed dealers; and the Altamont Pant and Glove Company, which offered limited employment on the county's west side. All other industries were in the county seat of Effingham. Quite important were the Feuerborn Church Furniture factory, Boos Block (manufacturer of meat-cutting blocks), Van Camp cannery, Pevely Dairy Company and Vulcan Last Plant, a wooden shoe-heel factory, on the city's south side. The last named manufacturer employed about three hundred workers in 1930. It was the county's largest employer.

The milk processing plant was the focus of a lot of unrest during the Depression years. Troubles developed in 1931 when Pevely cut milk prices. About one-third of the county's 1,500 dairy farmers joined the Sanitary Milk Producers Association (SMPA) and participated in a general milk strike that was spreading throughout the entire Midwest.

Violence erupted on several Effingham County rural roads as SMPA members set up roadblocks keeping nonmembers from taking milk into Pevely Dairy in Effingham. Milk houses were blown up, and Pevely truckers were harassed on their trip to St. Louis. Masked men hijacked several Pevely trucks, dumped the milk on the road and shot the trucks full of bullet holes. One farmer who refused to cooperate with the SMPA strikers left Effingham one afternoon and noticed that his car was sputtering. Stopping his car for a closer inspection revealed several sticks of dynamite had been wired to the chassis and the fuse lighted. Several local farmers were arrested by the county sheriff and arraigned before Effingham County judge Harold Taylor. They were all released on bail and eventually the charges were dropped.

Giving voice to the Effingham County farmers' concerns were a Catholic priest named Father Nell and Bliss Loy, a Methodist layman who was a resident of Loy Prairie. Together in Loy's Dodge, they traveled across the county, even speaking on WLS radio in Chicago. The strike continued into the fall of 1932, when an arbitration committee settled the controversy. Milk prices remained lower than when the strike had begun.

Other problems resulted from the hundreds of transients who were riding the rails into Effingham and begging for food. They camped at a place called "Bum's Roost" near the Vulcan Last Plant and on the dumping site just

Effingham County, Early 1900s Until Mid-Century

outside Edgewood where Chicago previously had dumped thousands of train carloads of trash. Fifty to sixty people were carried into the county on every freight train and offered to chop wood, beat rugs or do anything for a handout. Effingham earned the reputation of being a "Panhandler's Dream" and, with that, a number of problems.

Housewives complained about a menacing fellow they called "Jack the Grabber." A local doctor was called to treat several bums suffering stomach cramps who said they had eaten "Big-eyed Chick Stew." He didn't know what that was, and they told him it was a great horned hoot owl. Police once found a dead tramp along the Illinois Central tracks, and once when a Shumway farmer refused to provide enough loose straw for a transient sleeping overnight in his hayloft, the man left angry the next morning, saying he was going back to Missouri where the decent folks live.

Feeding these transients became a problem for the city of Effingham. A businessman named Clarence Wyckoff formed the Goodfellows Club in 1931, which opened up a kitchen for them. Over five thousand meals (typically beans, coffee and day-old bread) were served at the Goodfellows Kitchen between 1931 and 1933, when the local relief project ran out of funds.

The milk strike and the transient problem were followed by the first real turning point in the Depression for Effingham County. General business volume dropped drastically for the first time in 1932 by about 20 percent. This was the year of the Black Depression for the United States, as unemployment reached twelve to fifteen million. But some local businessmen remained confident.

An area vending business, begun in 1928, sold enough peanuts and potato chips to permit the owners to buy a new Buick and new home in 1932. Goodfellows Club leader Clarence Wyckoff opened his new loan office in downtown Effingham. In that same year, however, work began to slow down at Vulcan Last. Jobs became scarce.

The year 1933 marked the second turning point, as the county for the first time in its history had to seek outside help for its unemployed. The Goodfellows Club closed its kitchen. Struggling with a $35,000 deficit and already one year behind in county spending, the Effingham County Board of Supervisors went to Springfield to apply for state aid from the Illinois Emergency Relief Commission (IERC). Created by Governor Henry Horner in 1933, the commission provided relief checks averaging $8.48 for a family of four. About one hundred families were immediately placed on the IERC relief rolls. Never during the Depression did more than 10 percent of the county receive IERC relief money.

President Franklin Delano Roosevelt's temporary work-relief program called the CWA (Civil Works Administration) employed four hundred Effingham County men during the winter of 1933–34 doing general road maintenance. Businesses also supported the National Recovery Administration (NRA) effort to shorten working hours to thirty-hour weeks, giving jobs to more people. NRA didn't really have much impact on local business.

Most important and beneficial was the WPA (Works Progress Administration), sometimes called by locals "We Piddle Around." Eleven WPA projects got underway in 1935 employing several men at $40 per month. Several roads were improved, including a cement highway between the villages of Shumway and Beecher City, new bridges, paved guttering and sidewalks. Workers set up a WPA library in Effingham, wrote a new county history and indexed twenty-two thousand items at the county courthouse. There was a WPA sewing room, a drama project and a craft shop with instruction in woodcraft, electricity and hobbies. Eight WPA basketball teams competed against one another in new WPA-built gyms at Watson, Mason and Dieterich. A similar New Deal program called the PWA (Public Works Administration) built new high schools at Beecher City and Dieterich. The PWA built the high school in Effingham at a cost of $250,000 to replace the crowded Central School. That last-named project kept one hundred men busy for two years.

Employment and income came in a variety of forms. About two hundred young men from Effingham County between ages eighteen and twenty-five received training at the CCC (Civilian Conservation Corps) camp in

Date molded into the side of the WPA Depression-era project, Effingham High School.

Effingham County, Early 1900s Until Mid-Century

Charleston and then went to Oregon and other states for forestry work. Demands for gloves from the WPA, PWA and CCC also brought expansion to the Illinois Glove Factory in the city of Effingham. New Deal money helped the farmers. Nursing their wounds from the 1931 milk war, they quickly got behind the AAA (Agricultural Adjustment Act) in 1933. Effingham County farm adviser Vernon Evans and the Farm Bureau signed up farmers for benefit payments that paid them to cut the number of acres in production. Nearly half of all local farmers signed up with the "Triple A" and received a total of $100,000 from the government in 1934.

One thousand farmers participated in the Soil Conservation program that replaced the previous AAA as land values plunged from fifty-two dollars an acre in 1925 to only thirty-nine dollars at the low point in the economic hard times. In 1940, land foreclosures rose only slightly and never reached crisis proportions. Governor Henry Horner received only five letters from Effingham County farmers asking for mortgage aid.

Hard work and sacrifice helped these farmers through as much as anything. Farm boys sometimes earned extra income from shucking corn in northern Illinois at two cents a bushel or working for the WPA and PWA. Some earned money by cutting wood and shipping it in boxcars to Indianapolis, receiving four dollars a load. Women worked as hard as the men. Eggs were traded in town for staples like sugar and flour, and fryers were sold to the city people. Breakfast often meant boiled wheat or corn mush.

Despite these hardships, things were looking up by 1936. Effingham County had passed the roughest times by then, with 95 percent of all property taxes reported paid by the county treasurer. No other Illinois county reported less unpaid taxes in 1936 than Effingham. County government began operating on a cash basis for the first time in eight years. But money for individuals was still hard to come by. One Effingham funeral home even sent a bill collector into the countryside to accept cows, hogs and even land for funeral bill settlements. People were willing to pay; they just didn't have the cash. Country doctors like Dr. Lorton of Shumway charged eighteen dollars to deliver a baby. One couple paid him fifteen dollars and a smoked ham. Another man came home and told his wife he had just paid the doctor ten dollars. She turned to him and said, "Two more payments and the baby will be ours."

Lifestyles definitely became simpler and more frugal. Meals often consisted of a single dish like mush or rice and milk and sometimes greens. People ate only at mealtimes, and no food was wasted. Meat was usually pork, very rarely beef. Most food was raised in the garden or on the farm. Canned foods seldom were bought from the grocery store. Milk was delivered by horse and wagon.

Picnics were fun for the whole family, and free movies provided the fun on Saturday night. Church socials kept many people busy, and church attendance stayed pretty much the same. Only a few new churches were built in the county, including St. John's Lutheran in Effingham in 1935 and First Baptist in Altamont.

Sports activities drew large crowds, especially the Effingham High School basketball games. There was no high school football until the 1940s, but students played a lot of baseball, tennis and track. Cross-country skiing was also popular.

Many adults found pleasure in the diversions of gambling, dancing and drinking. Teenagers and young adults paid thirty-five cents to attend the platform dances in Teutopolis and other towns. Neither the divorce rate nor the suicide rate changed significantly in the county. Perhaps the Depression pulled families closer together.

The recession that hit America in 1937 did not touch Effingham County. The main reason was the oil boom of 1937–40. Oilmen came from Oklahoma, including Joseph T. King, who had testified at the famous Teapot Dome Trials under the Harding administration of the early 1920s. Oil production centered south of Effingham on the village of Mason. Harold Taylor's title company became swamped with title transfer requests as the entire county was leased for mineral rights. Nearly two hundred new homes were built in Effingham to provide housing for the "oil johnnies." Their four-dollar-a-day salaries also boosted the local grocery and retailing trade. The Altamont Chamber of Commerce described the housing situation during the oil boom as "desperate" as property values and rents doubled within the three-year period. Prosperity was gradually returning to Effingham County as a result of all these activities. By 1939, the PWA and WPA could no longer find enough unemployed men to keep going. The Effingham County unemployment office reported the lowest number of compensation payments in the entire state. Vulcan Last kept 540 workers busy turning out four thousand pairs of shoe heels daily, and traveling salesmen often remarked that Effingham was the "best town in this part of Illinois."

By 1940, most Effingham County residents realized they had survived the Depression decade better than most. Voters rejected President Roosevelt, whose New Deal had helped them through. Fear of "creeping socialism" and a strong belief in the philosophy of "rugged individualism" turned many of them against FDR in the 1940 election. President Roosevelt carried

Effingham County, Early 1900s Until Mid-Century

the county by a mere forty-seven votes, in comparison to his landslide victory in 1932. By that election, however, another giant issue loomed—America's role in stopping the Axis Powers.

World War II did not witness the anti-German sentiment of the First World War. The same patriotic spirit inspired many to enlist. Service personnel from Effingham County were at Pearl Harbor witnessing and dying in the "Day of Infamy." From that point on, many who had grown up in the south central prairie of Illinois participated in every major theatre and battle of the war. An excellent account of their deeds is found in the book *They Served with Honor* and will not be detailed here. Suffice to say that once again there was great sacrifice on the part of county residents on the battlefields of the world.

The various monuments and walls of honors that are found in the communities scattered throughout the county pay tribute to all veterans, but especially to those who were part of the huge number who served in the struggle against forces that threatened the world during the Second World War. The people had been challenged, and they triumphed.

The spirit of determination that was typical of Effingham County during wartime had to be called upon once again before the decade of the 1940s

Edgewood American Legion post monument to honor all military veterans.

ended. Death and destruction came to the community in the form of a devastating fire. The story of the event and the county's response to it is a major chapter in the history of the area.

Engraved on the stone near the entry to the hospital are the words "SAINT ANTHONY'S MEMORIAL HOSPITAL ERECTED IN THE YEAR OF OUR LORD 1952." It is a sample declaration, but the story behind it is one of great triumph over the most tragic experience that the county has ever suffered.

To understand the depth of emotion, one has to travel backward in time to the night of April 4, 1949, a night in which there was an overwhelming sense of surrealism. The sky over the city of Effingham was a strange pink with orange color as a result of the fire that burned at the seventy-four-year-old building known as St. Anthony's Hospital. Sirens screamed during the night as fire departments from throughout the area rushed into the town to the scene of great disaster.

The destruction did not take long—only about ten minutes, in fact—as fire quickly spread through the hallways of the building that held 120 beds. Firemen from Effingham and surrounding communities fought the blaze for about three hours before they brought it under control; then came the task of searching for the dead.

That tragic evening there were 128 patients, staff and visitors in the building; 77 of them died in the fire. Temporary housing for rescued patients was quickly established, as was a morgue. There was also a headquarters for gathering information about the survivors and the deceased. Such headquarters, of course, was needed due to the confusion of the evening and the fact that many survivors were taken to other hospitals miles distant from Effingham County.

The emotion of the evening left its mark on the psyche of the area. The piteous screams of those who were burning or leaping from windows left a mark on the minds of people nearby, memories that could not be forgotten.

There were also many deeds of heroism and love that night that also became deeply imprinted memories on the people of the area. One of the finest statements of such was in the April 18, 1949 issue of *Life* magazine, which through its photography caught the great emotion that characterized the population of Effingham County. In a piece entitled "SORROW IN THE 'HEART OF THE USA,'" readers were allowed to see the grave concerns, emotion, anxiety and fears of area residents. Particularly moving were pictures such as the one of the Teutopolis school band standing in front of the burned hospital after the group had attended the funeral of one of its members; or of a man in the temporary morgue searching under the

Effingham County, Early 1900s Until Mid-Century

blankets for the remains of his six-week-old nephew, a youngster whose parents were too upset to search for themselves; or of a ten-year-old boy sitting in a church viewing the funeral being conducted for his father, a man who had died in a frantic attempt to rescue his wife, a hospital nurse. There were pictures of families completing their household routines even though loved ones had burned to death in the fire.

The *Life* magazine article told about the heroic efforts of many people. For example, one story dealt with a young nurse who died with ten babies in the nursery. "Fern Riley Was a Heroine" detailed how this quiet young woman, immediately after the fire broke out, was heard to say, "My babies! I've got to stay with my babies."

The casualties continued in the aftermath of the fire. One woman who had lost an eleven-year-old son in the blaze, after attending a solemn memorial service, died a few hours later from grief and shock.

The gruesome removal of bodies from the burned-out building continued in the days following the fire. But a spirit of renewal and hope swept throughout the county as people began to talk about the need to rebuild the hospital. Then, as the St. Anthony's Memorial Hospital Centennial Report later stated, "Out of the havoc, a community unites." By three o'clock in the morning during the night of the fire, a Protestant layman, J. William Everhart, paid a visit to the parish home of a Catholic priest to offer his services in the effort to rebuild the hospital. Within one hour, church and hospital officials accepted his generous proposal. Everhart became the chairman of the hospital finance committee.

Before the end of the same day, an enthusiastic organization, the Effingham Civic Foundation, had been assembled to spearhead the effort to get financial contributions from local citizens and to publicize the endeavor. There were scores of volunteers who mailed appeals by the thousands, as printers located up to 150 miles from the county produced flyers explaining the monetary needs.

Eventually, $125,000.00 came into the foundation's treasury from the greater Effingham area, as well as $406,527.67 from the forty-eight states that composed the United States at that time and from four foreign countries. Boy Scouts stood on street corners collecting funds. Especially significant, it seemed, was the impact of that *Life* magazine article in publicizing the tragedy and appealing to the generosity of the American public. Other dollars came from the federal government, the State of Illinois and the Hospital Sisters of the Third Order of St. Francis. The last-named group also financed the chapel and garage.

Effingham County

Sign on the Effingham County Courthouse lawn to show progress in fundraising for the new hospital.

St. Anthony's Memorial Hospital, Effingham.

Effingham County, Early 1900s Until Mid-Century

The groundbreaking ceremony for the new structure was on August 15, 1951, when the cornerstone was set in place in a solemn ceremony led by Bishop William A. O'Connor of Springfield. About one thousand people gathered for the event and listened attentively as a series of speakers told the story of the progress being made to rebuild.

When the dedication of the new hospital took place, on May 16, 1954, thousands came to the hospital grounds to hear Illinois governor William Stratton deliver the main address. To all who attended the event, it was evident that the area had united in triumphing over one of the great tragedies in the nation's history. From the ashes, a structure of great beauty had arisen. The building remains an object of great pride throughout the region. It is a symbol of the character of the people who have lived in the area since the first settlers moved onto the prairie in the first third of the nineteenth century.

LIST OF SOURCES

BOOKS AND BOOKLETS

Alvord, Clarence, ed. *Centennial History of Illinois*, vols. II and III. Springfield: Illinois Centennial Commission, 1920.

Bateman, Newton, and Paul Selby, eds. *Historical Encyclopedia of Illinois and History of Fayette County.* 2 vols. Chicago: Munsell Publishing, 1910.

———. *Illinois Historical Effingham County Biographical*. Chicago: Munsell Publishing Company, 1910.

Battle, J.H. *Counties of Cumberland, Jasper, and Richland, Illinois*. Chicago: F.A. Battey and Co., 1884.

Brink, I., ed. *History of Fayette County, Illinois*. Philadelphia: Brink, McDonough and Company, 1878.

Burtschi, Mary. *Vandalia: Wilderness Capital of Lincoln's Land*. Decatur, IL: Huston-Patterson Corporation, 1963.

Carpenter, Charles F., Secretary of State. *Illinois Blue Book 1959–1960*. Springfield: State of Illinois, 1959.

List of Sources

Centennial Book Committee. *Altamont Area Centennial 1871–1971*. Altamont, IL: 1971.

Centennial Committee. *A History of the First Christian Church 1867–1967*, Effingham, IL: 1967. Chicago: Lake City Publishing Company, 1893.

———. *Sigel Centennial 1863–1963*. N.p.: 1963.

Commissioner of Labor. "Illinois College of Photography, Effingham, Illinois." *Seventeenth Annual Report of the Commissioner of Labor, Trade and Technical Education*. Washington, D.C.: Government Printing Office, 1902.

Davis, J.W., et al. *Effingham County School History Centennial 1918*. 1918.

Feldhake, Hilda E., ed. *Effingham County Illinois—Past and Present*. Effingham, IL: Effingham Regional Historical Society, 1968.

Fiftieth Anniversary Souvenir of Effingham, Illinois 1853–1903. Effingham, IL: Effingham Democrat, 1903.

Filene, Catherine. *Careers for Women*. Boston: Houghton Mifflin Company, 1920.

Hammand, Lavern, ed. "Coles County in the Civil War." *Eastern Illinois University Bulletin* 234. Charleston: Eastern Illinois University, April 1961.

Historical Records Survey. *Inventory of the County Archives of Illinois: Effingham County, No. 25*. Chicago: Works Progress Administration, 1940.

History of Sangamon County, Illinois. Chicago: Inter-State Publishing Company, 1881.

Hospital Sisters of the Third Order of St. Francis. *St. Anthony Memorial Hospital Effingham, Illinois: Centennial Report 100 Years 1875–1975*. Effingham, IL: 1975.

Illinois College of Photography. Annual catalogue. 1905–6, Effingham, Illinois.

Jeiler, Ignatius. *The Venerable Mother Frances Schervier*. St. Louis, MO: B. Herder, 1895.

List of Sources

Lewis, Phil, et al. *Historical Postcards of Effingham County, Illinois.* Effingham, IL: Historical Collectors Association, 2003.

Lindvahl, Craig, ed. *They Served with Honor.* N.p.: 1996.

Lorton, Ethel Allsop. *Prairie Boy.* Teutopolis, IL: Worman Printery, 1968.

McCallen, A.D., ed. *Old Settlers' Annual and Homecoming Reunion 1912.* Effingham, IL: Lecrone Press, 1912.

Newcomb, Mary. *Four Years Personal Experience in the War.* Chicago: H.S. Mills & Co., Publishers, 1893.

Paxon, Frederic L. *History of the American Frontier.* Boston: Houghton-Mifflin, 1924.

Perrin, William H., ed. *History of Crawford and Clark Counties.* Chicago: O.L. Baskin and Company, 1883.

———. *History of Effingham County, Illinois.* Chicago: O.L. Baskin and Company, 1883.

Portrait and Biographical Record: Effingham, Jasper and Richland Counties Illinois. Chicago: Lake City Publishing Company, 1893.

Souvenier und Programm Der 15. General-Versammlung Des Deutschen Katholischen Vereins-Bundes von Illinois. N,p.: 1907

Spurlin, Charlotte, et al. *Edgewood Centennial History 1857–1957.* Edgewood, IL: Edgewood Lions Club, 1957.

Stanton, Carl. *They Called It Treason.* Bunker Hill, IL: 2002.

Teutopolis Centennial Souvenir Program and Historical Sketch. Teutopolis, IL: 1939.

Wood, Jennie, ed. *Memorial on the Life and Character of Hon. Benson Wood.* Robinson, IL: Argus Printing, 1916.

List of Sources

Newspapers

Alton [IL] *Telegraph*. "National Road Convention," July 26, 1839, 2.

Burlington [IA] *Weekly Hawk-Eye*. "A parcel of drunken copperheads…," April 1, 1863, 4.

Cedar Rapids [IA] *Evening Gazette*. "Photographers' State Meeting," April 18, 1903, 16.

Centralia [IL] *Sentinel*. "A Field Gone to Waste," November 30, 1865, 4.

———. "Funeral Obsequies and Sale of the Effects of the Deceased," November 20, 1865, 4.

———. "Our Home Rebels," August 18, 1864, 1.

Chicago Tribune. "A Letter from Yancey," May 20 1861, Letter to Editor, 1.

———. "Nathan Burgess, Justice Avenged," June 19, 1875, 1.

Daily Review [Decatur, IL]. "Prepare for Draft," June 7, 1917, 1.

Decatur [IL] *Review*. "Arcola Wreck Was Accidental," May 8, 1917, 2.

———. "Effingham Boy Dies in France," June 18, 1918, 2.

———. "Effingham Leads in W.S.S. Sales," July 2, 1918, 6.

———. "Effingham Women Raise $85 for Kits," September 28, 1917, 10.

———. "Former Effingham Man a Spy?," August 16, 1918, 7.

Dieterich [IL] *Gazette*. "Immense Throng Greets Bryan," October 18, 1906, 1.

Edwardsville [IL] *Intelligencer*. "Audacious Crime," July 14, 1875, 1.

Effingham [IA] *Democrat*. "Altgeld at Altamont," October 21, 1892, 1.

List of Sources

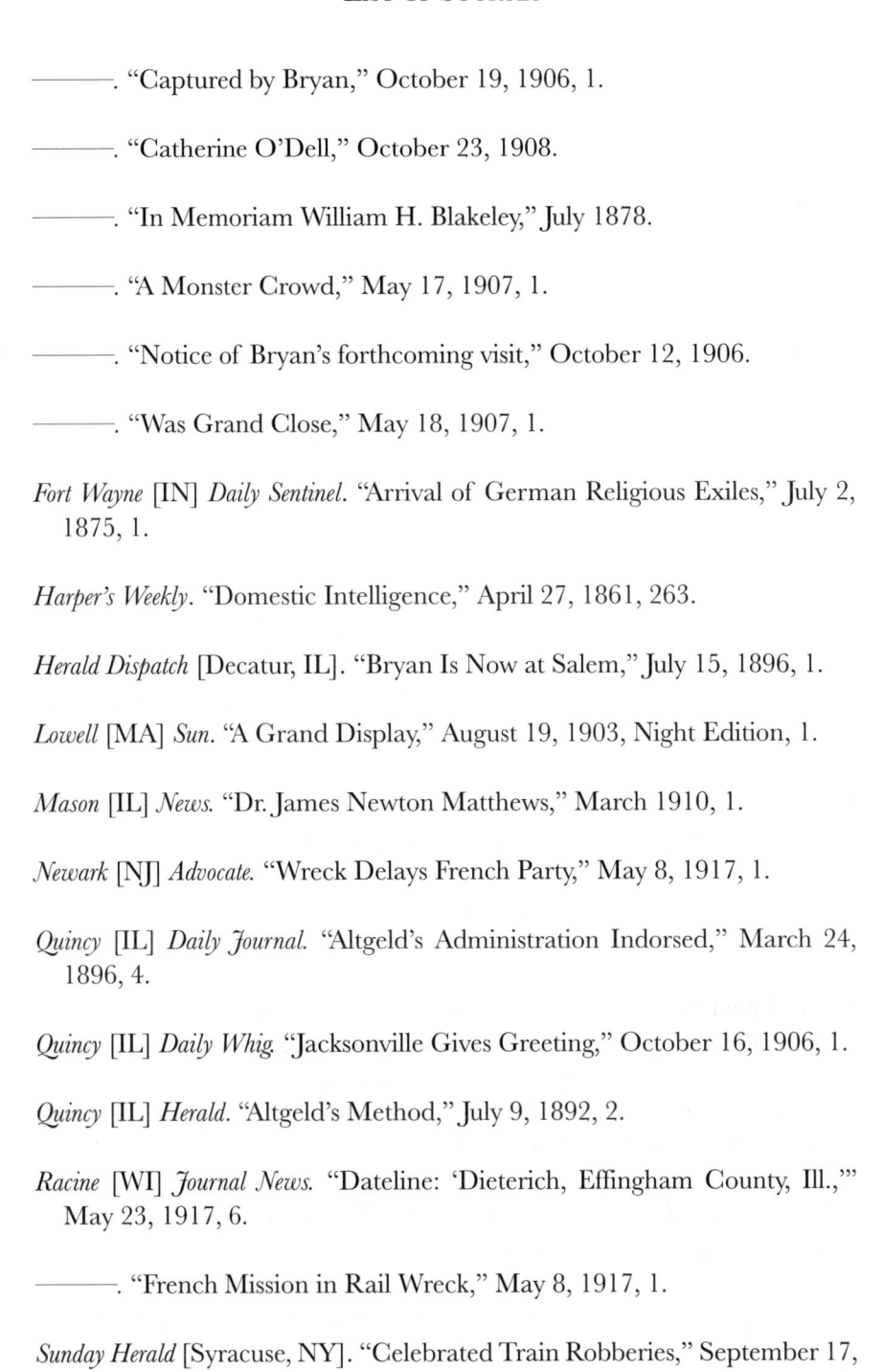

———. "Captured by Bryan," October 19, 1906, 1.

———. "Catherine O'Dell," October 23, 1908.

———. "In Memoriam William H. Blakeley," July 1878.

———. "A Monster Crowd," May 17, 1907, 1.

———. "Notice of Bryan's forthcoming visit," October 12, 1906.

———. "Was Grand Close," May 18, 1907, 1.

Fort Wayne [IN] *Daily Sentinel.* "Arrival of German Religious Exiles," July 2, 1875, 1.

Harper's Weekly. "Domestic Intelligence," April 27, 1861, 263.

Herald Dispatch [Decatur, IL]. "Bryan Is Now at Salem," July 15, 1896, 1.

Lowell [MA] *Sun.* "A Grand Display," August 19, 1903, Night Edition, 1.

Mason [IL] *News.* "Dr. James Newton Matthews," March 1910, 1.

Newark [NJ] *Advocate.* "Wreck Delays French Party," May 8, 1917, 1.

Quincy [IL] *Daily Journal.* "Altgeld's Administration Indorsed," March 24, 1896, 4.

Quincy [IL] *Daily Whig.* "Jacksonville Gives Greeting," October 16, 1906, 1.

Quincy [IL] *Herald.* "Altgeld's Method," July 9, 1892, 2.

Racine [WI] *Journal News.* "Dateline: 'Dieterich, Effingham County, Ill.,'" May 23, 1917, 6.

———. "French Mission in Rail Wreck," May 8, 1917, 1.

Sunday Herald [Syracuse, NY]. "Celebrated Train Robberies," September 17, 1893, 4.

LIST OF SOURCES

Teutopolis [IL] *Press*. "Civil War Experiences of Henry 'Soldier' Uptmor," n.d.

———. "Joseph Horn," January 28, 1904. Copy of newspaper clipping belonging to author.

———. "Notification about Bryan's visit," October 11, 1906.

Waterloo [IA] *Courier*. "X-Ray Discovers Needle," December 12, 1896, 6.

JOURNALS AND MAGAZINES

Bissellonian 1, no. 4 (March 1912).

Brotherhood of Locomotive Engineers Monthly Journal 9–10. "The Funeral of Milo E. Eames, the Murdered Engineer" (September 1875): 487–89.

———. 9–10. "Murder of Brother Milo Eames of Effingham Division No. 181" (August 1875): 427–28.

Donaldson, Delaine. "Lewis H. Bissell's World-Famous Photography College." *Historic Illinois* 31, no. 6 (April 2009): 3–5.

———. "Willkommen Delegaten: The 1907 German Catholic Convention in Effingham." *Historic Illinois* 32, no. 3 (October 2009): 12–14.

Gustorf, Frederick. "Frontier Perils Told by an Early Illinois Visitor." *Journal of the Illinois State Historical Society* 55 (Summer 1962): 136–56.

Hardin, Thomas L. "The National Road in Illinois." *Journal of the Illinois State Historical Society* 60 (Spring 1967): 5–22.

Illinois Catholic Historical Review 3, no. 1. "The Franciscans in Southern Illinois" (July 1920): 260–67.

Life Magazine. "Sorrow in the 'Heart of the USA,'" April 18, 1949: 29–33.

Munsey's Magazine 26, no. 6. "Advertising section" (March 1902): 918.

List of Sources

Photographic Times-Bulletin 34. "Notes and News" (1902): 91–92.

Plassmeyer, Theodore. "Propaganda Foiled: A Contribution to the Study of Prejudice and Intolerance." *Social Justice Review* (April 1949): 25–28; (May 1949): 60–64; (June 1949): 96–98; (July–August 1949): 132–35; (September 1949): 167–70; (October 1949): 203–6; (November 1949): 239–43; (December 1949): 276–79; (January 1950): 312–14; (February 1950): 348–50; (March 1950): 385–89; (April 1950): 25–29; (May 1950): 61–64; (June 1950): 96–100; (July–August 1950): 132–35; (September 1950): 168–70; (October 1950): 204–6; (November 1950): 238–42; (December 1950): 276–78.

Russ, J.H. "From Rev. J.H. Russ, Ewington, Effingham Co." *Home Missionary* 25 (1853): 190.

St. Louis and Canadian Photographer 24. "Editorial Chit-Chat" (1900): 484.

U.S. Congress, House. House Committee on Roads and Canals. A Report of the Commissioner Appointed to Lay Out the Cumberland Road from Zanesville, in the State of Ohio, to Seat of Government in the State of Missouri. Document 113, 20th Congress, 2nd session, 1829.

———. Inspection Cumberland Road and Its Concerns in 1833. Document 417. 23rd Congress, 1st Session, 1834.

Wilson's Photographic Magazine 40, no. 583. "Editor's Table" (1903): 531.

Unpublished Manuscripts and Audio Tape

Allen, Edward. Script for an Effingham High School Illinois History class slide presentation about Effingham County during the Great Depression, 1981.

Collection of essays written about the American Civil War by Effingham County students for a contest sponsored by the Effingham Regional Historical Society in cooperation with the Effingham County Superintendant of Schools, 1961.

List of Sources

Davis, Zona B. Taped Interview for an Effingham High School Illinois History class, 1981.

Shriver, Joseph. *Notebook of the Survey for Location of the Cumberland Road between Terre Haute, Ind. and St. Louis, Mo.* Missouri Historical Society, St. Louis.

William, Wilson. *Autobiography*, 1866. Helen Matthes Library, Genealogical and Historical Society section, Effingham, Illinois.

Wright, Charles M., III. *The Wright House in Altamont, Illinois.* June 1981 (Rev. June 1984). The Wright House, Altamont, Illinois.

Wright, Dr. Charles M., III, ed. *From Day Books of Dr. Charles M. Wright of Freemanton, Effingham County, Illinois 1858–1869.* Helen Matthes Library, Effingham, Illinois, Genealogical and Historical Society section.

Wright, H.H. *Recollections*, c. 1906. Helen Matthes Library, Effingham, Illinois.

ABOUT THE AUTHOR

Delaine Donaldson is a retired educator with thirty-five years of experience at Effingham High School in Effingham, Illinois, and forty-one as an adjunct social studies department faculty member for Lake Land College of Mattoon, Illinois. He is the recipient of numerous teaching awards, including two from the State Board of Education—an Award of Merit during the 1991-92 school year and an Award of Recognition during the 1994-95 school year—and the National Daughters of Colonial Wars Illinois state teacher award in 1991. In 2005, he was honored as one of fifty outstanding alumni from Eastern Illinois University's graduate program during its first fifty years of existence, where he received both his undergraduate and graduate in history. He is a regular contributor of local history articles to area newspapers. He has had a monthly radio presentation about local history on an Effingham radio station; serves as the coordinator of a local historical lecture series dealing with Effingham County history; and is chairman of the Board of the Effingham County Cultural Center and Museum Association, Inc.

Visit us at
www.historypress.net